Praise *for* Dennis Lee

"Canada has produced many competent poets but few absolute masters.... *The Gods* confirms the presence of a master: Dennis Lee."
— MARK ABLEY, *Maclean's*

"Lee, like every great poet, cannot be catalogued or filed under any given poetic category. He is an exponent of the real; his lines are essentially prophetic."
— GWENDOLYN MACEWEN

"The trouble with Dennis Lee's children's rhymes is that they are unforgettable." — MARGARET ATWOOD

"One of the finest poets in the English language." — *Quill & Quire*

"One of the most important books of poetry in our country."
— ELI MANDEL, on *Civil Elegies*

"An astonishing batch of poems – unwieldy, tough-minded, shot through with passages of knotty and uncompromising beauty."
— PERRY NODELMAN, *Winnipeg Free Press*, reviewing *Civil Elegies*

"Being a citizen is hard, Lee tells us; love is hard, he also tells us. Being alive and having to look at yourself in the mirror is painful. But when all of this is accepted and lived with, it is still possible to affirm your right to be here and to state your case. Lee states his with unique eloquence."
— ROBERT FULFORD, *Toronto Star*

"*Civil Elegies* is our *Waste Land*.... It gave the city and the nation a sacramental landmark for a secular age." — NICK MOUNT

"Dennis Lee's poems are important to me above all because, more consistently than those of anyone else whose work I know, they manifest a full awareness of the poem as a form of musical score." — DENISE LEVERTOV, *Descant*

"The poems in *Riffs* are honest, passionate and full of insight. Their masterful rhythms and melodies re-establish Lee as one of the country's great poets."
— *Montreal Gazette*

"Impossible to put down. Lee has a way of making language seem inevitable.... Whether the emotional moment swoops or falls, we are taken along for the ride in an entirely convincing, captivating way."
— *Quill & Quire*, reviewing *Riffs*

"Lee resurrects the music of Dylan Thomas, the wordplay of e.e. cummings, the zany delight of his own *Alligator Pie*." — *Ottawa Citizen*, reviewing *Riffs*

"Poet Dennis Lee may add love-junkie beatnik of distinction to his long list of credentials." — *NOW Magazine*, reviewing *Riffs*

"Dennis Lee is the poet laureate of the Canadian kids' world."
— *Montreal Gazette*

"*Un* is a hair-raising yikes of a book.... There is dread, urgency, anger, nostalgia, and fear, but also a howling love for the world."
— KAREN SOLIE, *Globe and Mail*

"*Un* reconfigures English into something as weirdly expressive as it is resistant to paraphrase ... part jazz, part wolf howl, invoking no less than the end of the world." — ROBYN SARAH, *National Post*

"From Yeats through *Finnegans Wake*, from Dylan Thomas to Samuel Beckett, Lee hints at a long lineage of inventive writers whose work appeals to the ear as well as the mind." — *Quill & Quire*, reviewing *Un*

"*Yesno* is a masterwork." — MARK DICKINSON, *Malahat Review*

"This is wild, brave, urgent poetry, not quite like anything else being written; it has no truck with cheap grace or obvious answers, but is a singular, memorable, and necessary book."
— MAGGIE HELWIG, *Globe and Mail*, reviewing *Yesno*

"*Testament* spectacularly channels the inconceivable ... [a] great work."
— *Telegraph Journal*

"One of the most extraordinary bodies of work in contemporary English poetry." — PAUL VERMEERSCH

Dennis Lee
Heart Residence
Collected Poems
1967–2017

POETRY

Kingdom of Absence · 1967
Civil Elegies · 1968
Civil Elegies and Other Poems · 1972, 2012
The Death of Harold Ladoo [chapbook] · 1976
Miscellany [chapbook] · 1977
The Gods [chapbook] · 1978
The Gods · 1979
Riffs · 1982, 1993, 2015
The Difficulty of Living on Other Planets · 1987
Nightwatch: New and Selected Poems · 1996
Un · 2003
Yesno · 2007
The Bard of the Universe [chapbook] · 2007
Testament · 2012
Heart Residence: Collected Poems 1967–2017 · 2017

PROSE

Savage Fields: An Essay in Literature and Cosmology · 1977
Reading Adonis [chapbook] · 1987
Body Music: Essays · 1998
Re-Greening the Undermusic · 2016

IN TRANSLATION

Elégies civiles et autres poèmes · 1980
Pasticcio di alligatore e altre poesie · 2002
Ragoût de crocodile · 2005
Dimora del cuore / Heart Residence · 2006

DENNIS LEE

Heart Residence

Collected Poems · 1967–2017

ANANSI

Published in Canada in 2017 and the USA in 2017 by House of Anansi Press Inc.

www.houseofanansi.com

21 20 19 18 17   1 2 3 4 5

Library and Archives Canada
Cataloguing in Publication Data

Lee, Dennis, 1939–
[Poems]
  Heart residence : collected poems
  1967–2017 / Dennis Lee.

Issued in print and electronic formats.
ISBN 978-1-4870-0150-6 (hardback).
— ISBN 978-1-4870-0149-0
(paperback).
— ISBN 978-1-4870-0151-3 (pdf)

  I. Title. II. Title: Poems.

PS8523.E3 2017   C811'.54
  C2016-901827-X

C2016-901828-8

Library of Congress Control Number
  2016958366

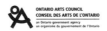

Canada Council   Conseil des Arts
for the Arts   du Canada

ONTARIO ARTS COUNCIL
CONSEIL DES ARTS DE L'ONTARIO
an Ontario government agency
un organisme du gouvernement de l'Ontario

We acknowledge for their financial support of our publishing program the Canada Council for the Arts, the Ontario Arts Council, and the Government of Canada through the Canada Book Fund.

Printed and bound in Canada

Editor's Foreword

For eight straight years of crud in public places
we worked to incite a country to belong to....
— "The Death of Harold Ladoo"

Poets are often solitary and socially awkward creatures, uncertain or forgetful of what communities they belong to. You could not say that of Dennis Lee, who has a keen sense of social responsibility and a deadly earnest political sense to go with it. This is crucial to the kinds of poet he is – and he is several quite different kinds of poet at once.

It isn't unheard of for several poets to inhabit the same body. During two fervent decades the great poet of modern Lisbon, Fernando Pessoa, wrote four very different bodies of work under four different names, and occasional works under fifty or sixty additional names. T. S. Eliot wrote not only *Four Quartets* but also some droll musical comedy and *Old Possum's Book of Practical Cats*. Lee has turned out to be one of the world's very few truly mature political poets, the city of Toronto's *de facto* (and formerly *de jure*) poet laureate, a wonderfully zany lyricist and rhymester for adults and children, and Canada's most articulate poet of full-frontal physical love. But unlike Pessoa, he has pursued his various roles under only one name. Different though they are, the several poets called Dennis Lee have a massive common root – and like the limbs of a big tree, they form a single, integral shape.

This, I believe, is the first of his many books in which that integral shape is made clear.

Lee's complete poems, which will surely be published some day, will make a thicker book than this one. Its overall shape may therefore be more difficult to discern, but I believe it will be essentially the same shape we see here: the natural order of what he has made. He has been from the outset a poet who writes books, not single poems. Writing books involves as much pruning as planting – and the purpose of pruning is not to make shrubs look like leaf-bearing urns, green polyhedrons, or vegetable teddy bears, but to elucidate a shape that is truly their own. It does not surprise me that Lee's books of poems, many and different though they are, turn out to be one book, but it has given me real pleasure to work alongside him, doing the minimal clipping and weeding required to prove that this is so.

The architecture matters because it is a measure of Lee's artistry and a landmark that the rest of us can use to find our way. It also matters because it clarifies the integrity of his lifelong task. The goofy rhymester, the subtle lyricist, the poet of carnal love, and the elegiac, hardcore political thinker are all engaged in the same project. They are out to build a city, a country, a world, in which humans are nourished instead of stunted by their culture – and are thereby enabled to nurture instead of destroy the planet they live on. This is poetry that matters, though by no means all of it sounds grave.

Except for a few pages of new work and a single cluster of translations, everything here comes from one of those books that Lee has crafted over the years. There are unpublished poems and cantatas; there are also uncollected poems, songs, and additional translations that have appeared in periodicals or been performed on television or the stage – but if they had not entered into the fabric of one of Lee's previous books, we did not try to weave them into this one.

Even his first book, *Kingdom of Absence* – the House of Anansi's first publication, issued half a century ago – was conceived and constructed as an architectural entity, not a mere collection of poems. The essential subject of that book – the moral and metaphysical emptiness at the heart of modern life – has remained one of Lee's abiding concerns, though by the time the work was printed he had already outgrown the voice in which it was written. The brief selection included here marks the first time he has permitted any part of *Kingdom of Absence* to be republished. Each of his subsequent major poems or sequences for adult readers – *Civil Elegies, The Death of Harold Ladoo, Riffs, Nightwatch,* and *Testament* – is here in its entirety, and each of these five seems to me an essential part of the overall shape I have mentioned.

Lee has made a habit of revisiting these works, revising the published versions, sometimes substantially and repeatedly. *Civil Elegies*, issued first as a group of seven meditations, reappeared four years later as a group of nine. *Riffs* took a decade to find its blues-piano-centred form as a sequence of 88 asymmetrical licks. (Lee is a pianist; 88 is the number of black and white keys on a standard piano keyboard.) *Testament* – that late political poem in which language itself is pulled up by the roots in a search for non-anthropocentric moral foundations – also took ten years to settle down. It therefore seems worth noting that only two of these five structural pillars, *Ladoo* and *Nightwatch*, have been revised yet again for this publication.

There is now also a sixth structural pillar, entitled *Not Abstract Harmonies But*. It has come together slowly over many years, and its shape is visible here for the first time. A number of Lee's best-loved individual lyrics and elegies – "400: Coming Home," "Words for the Given," "Sibelius Park," "The Gods," "Coming Becomes You," as well as the title poem – are parts of this slow-growing sequence.

I will not claim that the section *"I Didn't Write This Poem by Myself"* is structurally crucial to the book, but it is part of the design. It consists of Lee's English versions of poems composed in Hungarian by György Faludy. Though he was born and died in Budapest, Faludy was one of the liveliest minds in Toronto during the 1970s and 1980s. Lee was one of many Canadian poets who joined the campaign to make English versions of Faludy's poems during those years – and for Lee that project too had a political dimension. Politics, when humanely conceived and practised, is not a mode of social combat; it is friendship on a systematic scale. It was crucial to Lee's vision of Toronto that the city should offer not just refuge but genuine hospitality to Faludy and the passionate cosmopolitanism he stood for.

Lee's poetry for children is part of the structure too. But while "poetry for children" is a useful tag, it is porous as a category. Few of the best poems for children are for children only. There are also sections of this book (*The Cat and the Wizard*; *The Mouse and the Maid*) where the distinction "for kids" or "for grown-ups" just doesn't apply – any more than it does with genuine folktales.

Lee was a child himself when he began to publish poems.[1] He also started to make books of poems for children almost as soon as he started making them for adults.[2] This branch of his work is not just part of the large structure; it is part of the deep foundation. Are the children's poems political as well? I think they are – in several senses. First, they are full of joy, and joy can have great political ramifications. They are also full of honest puzzlement at the otherness of others and the multiplicity of being. Much of their joy, though not all of it, is linguistic; it consists in cavorting with vowels and consonants and potato-racing with placenames. So the poems hold language in general up to a joyful standard. They also do not lie and claim that joy is all there is. Yet they prove, again and again, that joy is more nourishing than anger or despair – and they hint at the kind of steady work involved in nudging the balance in a happier direction. In all these respects, Lee's poems for children are close to his poems of physical love. The latter, in fact, have grown out of the former.

"What I want from a book," he has written, "is that it be a birthday party, to which all our selves are invited."[3] There it is again, at ground level: friendship on a systematic scale. Can a children's party serve as a cultural as well as a literary model? What else do we need from a civilization but that it be a celebration of being in the world – one to which all individuals and species are invited?

ROBERT BRINGHURST

---

1 A distinctly Leesian poem entitled "If" appears in the March 1948 issue of *Wee Wisdom* (published in Kansas City). Lee was seven when it was written, eight when it was printed.

2 The mimeographed preliminary edition of *Wiggle to the Laundromat* carries no date. It was probably published late in 1967 (the same year as *Kingdom of Absence*), and in any case no later than early 1968.

3 "Roots and Play," in *Body Music* (Anansi, 1998): 30.

Heart Residence
Collected Poems

for Susan

CONTENTS

THE DEATH OF HAROLD LADOO (1976, 1979)

THE CAT AND THE WIZARD (1967–2007)

"I DIDN'T WRITE THIS POEM BY MYSELF":
Translations from George Faludy (1978–85)

from SO COOL (2004)

RIFFS (1982, 1993, 1996)

THE MOUSE AND THE MAID (1987)

NOT ABSTRACT HARMONIES BUT

—— Part I (1972) ——

from

Kingdom of Absence

VI

The great constructs of the mind recede,
    wrenched out of focus.
Time slides, and the hammered glory of built cities
    lurches from ken. They stop mattering.

Rome fell, and London fell. New York
    is falling down and people build museums.
What will not go in cases is the people,
    squatting in the wreckage of the mind.

It is our dispensation that we live
    in havoc of a mighty city, once
the wonder of the world, now condemned.
    I know a few who, strung up in the city,
numb, bemused or raging, pitch their lives
    among that wrack and colonize the void.

IX

Loony with sunlight, Van Gogh stood and stared
into the wicker inferno, and stared until
those manic eyeballs blazed in contemplation.
What made a dowdy chair become volcanic?

The sun, the old implosion of the sun
that burst the churches' ken, and now has crept
into the wicker companion; before it attacks
paint, or you will be destroyed!

To see in a cosmos gone askew
is torment. A sudden chair may strike
for the jugular and the old palpable things
no longer mediate, they offer shards
and longing. How should stable men endure
mere energy, crammed naked into flowers?

XXX

I seen a
thirty dirty ladies on a pink kazoo
interdigitating while they masticated glue.
I did not know their surnames, I could not speak first
but I was laughing, and they sure looked fine.

And I got a lot of kicks, because the ladies burped out loud.
Then they all took out their dentures and I saw into their mouths.
They interlinked their fingers just like dancing ladies do
and they kissed each other's armpits while they sang God Save the Queen.

If I could only get untangled I'd be swinging like a pro.
I bet they'd really like me if my cords were OK.
I thought I tied a reef knot. I guess I was wrong.
So long sweet ladies! demoiselles, so long.

I am hanging by the short ones with nirvana on my mind.
And I'm laughing, and it all looks fine.

XXXVI

How often, in Muskoka, bedded down
    at midnight, in the heavy dark, distraught,
constrained by silence, the tough, unsundered
    long and preternatural northern calm,
as a single outboard inched across my hearing,
    fretting the lake, and the early
tremendum
    occurred, the soundless implosion in which I writhed;
and my wife's body moaned as it swerved through its dream;
    and the zero calm resounded; have I, still
baffled, resumed the shreds of my being, and named
    the name I could not speak, and called
to myself, as the night sounds once more inched across the silence,
    "Yes. It is the void. Can you rejoice?"

XXXVII

Yes. Only in this absence. When the spring
returns to blubbered streets, and sparrows cry
their pipsqueak hallelujahs, when the air
is warm and tickling on the wakened skin –
but only in this absence. When the cloud
of amiable trivia that bewitch the eye
or touch, or lover's whimsy, that bemuse
the father's anguish in his frolic child,
delights – then only in this poverty
and absence can the simple-witted spring
achieve right flowers in the fetid concrete,

or lovers do their bughouse in the mind.
And while such radiance fades, it has defined
the simple celebration of what is.

XXXVIII

There is a route of secular purgation,
the way of unmeaning, in whose steps many lag.
And it is hard, for naughting every tie
and sweetness one must come to love the void.

I do not say this wanting then to say
you quarry God. You do not quarry God.
Only the awkward darkness of unmeaning
lights you on your stationary way.

Over and over this is where you graze off
sideways, into masturbatory visions,
puppy-love for great ones, luxury,
indulgence, glamour, flips and letdowns, cant,
recanting, doubt, self-cancelling decisions,
and all the dead-end shortcuts of the way.

XLIII

Cities of light, and every time
    I belted off to city, bearing
limbo, limbo, lethal ambience
    another flicky powerpoint was gone.

Paris, Rome, Vienna
    incandescents.
Such civil light transfigures all that it transfigures
    yet does not me, o luminous, you guttering.

Song I thirst for grunts like prose; among the flimsy
    fables of the real I want
a factive, brute and palpable abyss.
    And therefore I demolish what I am
or long to be, pure dark incarnate outcry,
    and I make my city's mawkish human cries.

Civil Elegies

Man is by nature a political animal, and to know
that citizenship is an impossibility is to be cut off
from one of the highest forms of life.

— GEORGE GRANT

Do not cling to the notion of emptiness:
Consider all things alike. My friend,
There is only one word that I know now,
And I do not know its name.

— SARAHA

Toronto's New City Hall opened in 1965.
Two curved white towers gave onto a great
square; at the time, such a dramatic public
space was new in Toronto.

1

Often I sit in the sun and brooding over the city, always
in airborne shapes among the pollution I hear them, returning:
pouring across the square
in fetid descent they darken the towers
and the wind-swept place of meeting, and whenever
the thick air clogs my breathing it teems with their presence.
Many were born in Canada, and living unlived lives they died
of course but died truncated, stunted, never at
home in native space and not yet
citizens of a human body of kind. And it is Canada
that specialized in this deprivation. Therefore the spectres arrive,
    congregating
in bitter droves, thick in the April sunlight,
accusing us and we are no different, though you would not expect
the furies assembled in hogtown and ring me round, invisible, demanding
what time of our lives we wait for till we shall start to be.
Until they come the wide square stretches out
serene, and singly by moments it takes us in, each one for now
a passionate civil man – until it
sends us back to the acres of gutted intentions,
back to the concrete debris, to parking scars and the four-square tiers
of squat and righteous lives. And here
once more, I watch the homing furies' arrival.

I sat one morning by the Moore, off to the west
ten yards, and saw though diffident my city nailed against the sky
in ordinary glory.
And dreamed a better past. A place, a making,
two towers, a teeming, a genesis, a city.
And the men and women performed their daily lives
by ancient measure, patricians in muddy York,
and made their compact together against the gangs of the new.

And as that crumpled before the shambling onset, again the
lives we had not lived in phalanx invisibly staining
the square and vistas, casting back I saw
regeneration twirl its blood and the rebels riding
riderless down Yonge Street, plain men much
goaded by privilege – our other origin, and cried,
"Mackenzie knows a word! Mackenzie
knows a meaning!" but it was not true. Eight-hundred-odd steely insurgents
turned tail at the cabbage patch when a couple of bullets fizzed
and the loyalists, scared skinny by the sound of their own gunfire,
gawked and bolted south to the fort like rabbits,
the rebels for their part bolting north to the pub: the first
spontaneous mutual retreat in the history of warfare.
Canadians, in flight.

Buildings oppress me, and the sky-concealing wires
bunch zigzag through the air. I know
the dead persist in
by-laws, roadways, porticoes – the city I live in
is clogged with their presence; they
dawdle about in our lives and form a destiny, still
incomplete, still dead weight, still
demanding whether Canada will be.

But the mad bomber, Chartier of Major Street, Chartier
said it: that if a country has no living past to learn from,
neither is it a country, and promptly
blew himself to bits in the parliament john, leaving as civil testament
assorted chunks of prophet, twitching and
bobbing to rest in the flush.
And what can anyone do in this country, baffled and
making our penance for ancestors, what did they leave us? Indian-swindlers,
stewards of unclaimed earth and rootless what does it matter if they, our

forebears' flesh and bone were often
good men? Good men do not matter to history.
And what can we do here now, for at last we have no notion
what we might have come to be in America, alternative, and how make
	public
a presence which is not sold out utterly to the modern? utterly? to the
savage inflictions of what is for real, it pays off, it is only
accidentally less than human?

In the city I long for, green trees still
asphyxiate. The crowds emerge at five from jobs
that rankle and lag. Heavy developers
pay off aldermen still; the craft of neighbourhood,
its whichway streets and generations
anger the planners, they go on jamming maps
with asphalt panaceas; single men
still eke out evenings courting, in rooms, alone.
A man could spend a lifetime looking for
peace in that city. And the lives give way around him – marriages
founder, neighbourhoods sag – until
the emptiness comes down on him to stay.
But in the city I long for, the people complete
their origins. Among the tangle of
hydro, hydrants, second mortgages, amid
the itch for new debentures, greater expressways,
in sober alarm they jam their works of progress, asking where in truth
they come from and to whom they must belong.
And thus they clear a space in which
the full desires of those that begot them, great animating desires
that shrank and grew hectic as the land pre-empted their lives
might still take root, which eddy now and
drift in the square, being neither alive nor dead.
And the people accept a flawed inheritance

and they give it a place in their midst, forfeiting progress, forfeiting
dollars, forfeiting yankee visions of cities that in time it might grow
whole at last in their lives, they might
belong once more to their forebears, becoming their own men.

To be our own men! in dread to live
the land, our own harsh country, beloved, the prairie, the foothills –
and for me it is lake by rapids by stream-fed lake, threading
north through the terminal vistas of black spruce, in a
bitter, cherished land it is farm after
farm in the waste of the continental outcrop –
for me it is Shield but wherever terrain informs our lives and claims us;
and then, no longer haunted by
unlived presence, to live the cities:
to furnish, out of the traffic and smog and the shambles of dead precursors,
a civil habitation that is
human, and our own.

The spectres drift across the square in rows.
How empire permeates! And we sit down
in Nathan Phillips Square, among the sun,
as if our lives were real.
Headlines! high-rise! neon hieroglyphics!
And the towers' luminous sign, that not
one countryman has learned, that
men and women live that
they may make that
life worth dying. Living. Hey,
the dead ones! Gentlemen, generations of
acquiescent spectres gawk at the chrome
on American cars on Queen Street, gawk and slump and retreat.
And over the square where I sit, congregating above the Archer
they crowd in a dense baffled throng and the sun does not shine through.

2

Master and Lord, where
are you?
A man moves back and forth
between what must be done to save the world
and what will save his soul,
and neither is real. For many years
I could not speak your name, nor now but
even stilled at times by openings like
joy my whole life
aches, the streets I walk along to work declare
your absence, the headlines
declare it, the nation, and
over and over the harried lives I
watch and live with, holding my breath and
sometimes a thing rings true –
they all give way and declare your real absence.

Master and Lord,
let be. I can say
nothing about you that does not
vanish like tap water.
I know,
the world is not enough; a woman straightens
and turns from the sink and asks her life the question, why should she
fake it? – and after a moment she
shrugs, and returns to the sink. A man's
adrenalin takes hold, at a meeting he makes
his point, and pushes and sees that
things will happen now, and then in the pause he knows
there are endless things in the world and this is not for real.

Whatever is lovely, whatever deserves
contempt, whatever dies –
over and over, in every thing we meet
we meet that emptiness.
It is a homecoming, as men once knew
their lives took place in you.
And we cannot get on, no matter how we
rearrange our lives and we cannot let go for
then there is nothing at all.

Master and Lord, there was a
measure once.
There was a time when men could say
my life, my job, my home
and still feel clean.
The poets spoke of earth and heaven. There were no symbols.

3

The light rides easy on people dozing at noon in Toronto, or
here it does, in the square, with the white spray hanging
upward in plumes on the face of the pool, and the kids and the thrum of
    the traffic,
and the people come and they feel no consternation, dozing at
lunchtime; even the towers comply.
And they prevail in their placid continuance, idly unwrapping their food
day after day on the slabs by the pool, warm in the summer sun.
Day after day the light rides easy.
Nothing is important.
But once at noon I felt my body's pulse contract and
balk in the space of the square, it puckered and jammed till nothing

worked – the whole brave willed design
an abstract pass at grandeur, and casting back and forth
the only resonance that held was in the Archer.
Great bronze simplicity! that muscled form still
moved in the aimless expanse, and tense and
waiting to the south I stood until the clangor in my forearms found its
    outlet.
And when it came I knew that stark heraldic form is not
great art. For it is real, great art is less than its necessity.
But it held; when the monumental space of the square
went slack, it moved in sterner space.
Was shaped by earlier space and it ripples with
wrenched stress, the bronze is flexed by
blind aeonic throes
that bred and met in slow enormous impact,
and they are still at large for the force in the bronze churns
through it, and lunges beyond and also the Archer declares
that space is primal, raw, beyond control and drives toward a
living stillness, its own.

But if some man by the pool, doing his workaday
job in the city, hammering
type for credits or bread, or in for the day, wiped out in Long Branch
by the indelible sting of household acts of war,
or whatever; if a man strays into that
vast barbaric space it happens that he enters into
void and will go
under, or he must himself become void.

We live on occupied soil.
Across the barren Shield, immortal scrubland and our own,
where near the beginning the spasms of lava
settled to bedrock schist,

barbaric land, initial, our
own, scoured bare under
crush of the glacial recessions,
and later it broke the settlers, towing them
deeper and deeper each year beneath the
gritty sprinkle of soil, till men who had worked their farms for a lifetime
could snap in a month from simple cessation of will,
though the brute surroundings went on – the flagrant changes
of maple and sumach, the water in ripples of light,
the faces of outcrop, the stillness, and up the slopes
a vast incessant green that drew the mind
beyond its tether, north, to muskeg and
stunted hackmatack, and then the whine of icy tundra north to the pole –
despotic land, inhuman yet
our own, where else on earth? and reaping stone
from the bush their parents cleared, the sons gave
way and they drank all year, or went strange, or they sat and stared outside
as their cars settled back to slag and now what
races toward us on asphalt across the Shield –
by truck, by TV minds and the ore-bearing boxcars –
is torn from the land and all those fruitless lives, it no longer
stays for us, immemorial adversary, but is shipped and divvied abroad.

Take Tom Thomson, painter: he
did his work in the Shield.
Could guide with a blindfold on. Was part of the bush. Often when night
came down in a subtle rush and the scorched scrub still
ached for miles from the fires he paddled direct through
the palpable dark, hearing only the push and
drip of the blade for hours and then very suddenly the radiance of the
renewed land broke over his canvas. So. It was his
job. But no two moments land with the same sideswipe
and Thomson, for all his savvy, is very damp and
trundled by submarine currents, pecked by the fish out

somewhere cold in the Shield and the far loons percolate
high in November and he is not painting their cry.

Small things ignite us, and the quirky particulars
flare on all sides.
A cluster of birches, in moonlight;
a jack pine, gnarled and
focusing heaven and earth –
these might fend off void.
Or under the poolside arches the sunlight, skidding on paper destroyers,
kindles a dazzle, skewing the sense. Like that. Any
combination of us and time can start the momentary
ignition. If only it were enough.
But it is two thousand years since Christ's corpse rose in a glory,
and now the shiny ascent is not for us, Thomson is
done and we cannot
malinger among the bygone acts of grace.
For many are called but none are chosen now, we are the evidence
for downward momentum, although despite our longing still
restrained within the real, as Thomson's body really did
decay and vying to praise him
we bicker about which grave the carcass fills.

New silences occur in the drone of the square's great spaces.
The light overbalances, shadows
appear, the people walk away.
But massy and knotted and still the Archer continues its space,
which violates our lives, and reminds us, and has no mercy upon us.
For a people which lays its whiskey and violent machines
on a land that is primal, and native, which takes that land in greedy
innocence but will not live it, which is not claimed by its own
and it sells that land off even before it has owned it,
traducing the immemorial pacts of men and earth, free and
beyond them, exempt by miracle from the fate of the race –

that people will botch its cities, its greatest squares
will mock its money and stature, and prising wide
a civil space to live in, by the grace of its own invention it will
fill that space with the artifacts of death.

On Queen Street, therefore, in Long Branch, wherever the
people have come upon it, say that the
news is as bad as we thought.
We have spent the bankroll; here, in this place,
it is time to honour the void.

4

Among the things which
hesitate to be, is void our
vocation? The houses on the street
hold back from us, across the welter of city blocks
old friendships keep stalling,
even the square falls away and the acts of our statesmen
will not come real though we long for it.
Dwelling among the
bruised and infinitely binding world
are we not meant to
relinquish it all, to begin at last
the one abundant psalm of letting be?

If only it
held. If only
here and now were not fastened so
deep in the flesh and goodbye, but how should a man,
alive and tied to the wreckage that surrounds him,
the poisoned air goodbye, goodbye the lakes,

the earth and precious habitat of species,
goodbye the grainy sense of place, worn down in
words and the local ways of peoples, goodbye the children returning
as strangers to their roots and generations,
and cities dying of concrete, city goodbye my city of passionate bickering
neighbourhoods the corner stores
all ghosts among the high-rise, like bewildered nations after their
surcease as boundaries
diminish to formalities on maps goodbye, so many
lives gone down the drain in the service of empire,
bombing its demon opponents though they bleed like men goodbye,
and not that all things die but that they die meanly, and
goodbye the lull of the sun in the square, goodbye and
goodbye the magisterial life of the mind, in the
domination of number every
excellent workaday thing all spirited
men and women ceaselessly jammed at their breaking
points goodbye who have such little time on earth and constantly fastened
how should a man stop caring?

And yet the death of lakes, the gutting of our self-respect,
even the passage of Canada –
these do not intrude such radical
bereavement merely to
etch us in figures of loss, to bid us declare
how painfully each passing brings us down.
Every thing we own will disappear; nothing
belongs to us, and
only that nothing is home.
And this is what the things were telling us: if we can
face the rigours of detachment, meaning our
life, our job, our home, permitting it to
break over us, letting it
bring us down till every

itch and twitch of attachment loses its purchase,
at the dead-end of desire and for some it will last
a month and for some ten years, at last we may
find ourselves in the midst of what abounds,
though that is not it but now we are set
free to cherish the world which has been stripped away by stages, and with no
reason the things are renewed: the people, Toronto, the elms
still greening in their blighted silhouettes – some dead some
burgeoning but none our property, and now they
move at last in the clearness of open space, within the
emptiness they move very cleanly in the vehement enjoyment of their bodies.

But what good is that in a nation of
losers and quislings? and for the few tenacious
citizens of a land that was never our own, watching the
ore and the oil and the shore-lines gutted
for dollars by men from abroad, watching Canadians
peddle their birthright and for these others, good
stateless men and women and may they go down in civil fury –
how should they clutch and fumble after beatitude, crouching for
years till emptiness renews an elm-tree,
and meanwhile the country is gone?
    I think much now of Garneau, master of emptiness,
who in the crowded streets of Montreal
saw not lost souls but a company of lost bodies, and
moving into himself gave thanks when he discovered
nothing but desert and void.
And I know that appetite in my own life,
at work, at home, in the square, and more insistent every day it forges
outward through the living will of the body,
straining to reach its ground, oblivion.
    But some face exile at home and sniping at corporations,
manic at times, and the patsies of empire their leaders lying for votes,

till the impotence floods in their veins, there is
shame abounding and sometimes a few good
gestures between the asphalt and sky that might have been
adequate once, and finally dying on occupied soil.
Yet still they take the world full force on their nerve ends, leaving the
bloody impress of their bodies face forward in time, and I believe
they will not go under until they have taken the measure of empire.

5

It would be better maybe if we could stop loving the children
and their delicate brawls, pelting across the square in tandem, deking
from cover to cover in raucous celebration and they are never
winded, bemusing us with the rites of our own
gone childhood; if only they stopped
mattering, the children, it might be possible, now
while the square lies stunned by noon.
What is real is fitful, and always the beautiful footholds
crumble the moment I set my mind aside, though the world does recur.
Better, I think, to avoid the snag of attachment – the headlong particulars
which perpetually sucker us in, until they
lose their animal purchase and cease to endorse us;
this awakens the ache of being, and once again the lonesome ego
sets out dragging its ignominious hankerings across the world,
which does not regard them.
Perhaps we should
bless what doesn't attach us, though I do not know
where we are to find nourishment.
      So, in the square, it is a
blessed humdrum; the kids climb over the Archer, and
the pool reflects the sky, and the people passing by,

who doze, and gently from above the visible pollutants descend,
coating the towers' sheath. Sometimes it
works but once in summer looking up I saw the noxious cloud suspended
taut above the city, clenched, as now everywhere it is the
imperial way of life that bestows its fallout. And it did not
stay inert, but across the fabled horizon of Bay Street they came riding,
the liberators, the deputies of Jesus, the Marines, and had released
bacterial missiles over the Golden Horseshoe for love of all mankind,
and I saw my people streaming after calling welcome for the small change,
and I ran in my mind crying humiliation upon the country, as now I do also
    for it is
hard to stay at the surface one more time, with a queasy hi and goodbye to
    the char-broiled tykes of the Mekong Delta,
although the pool
reflects the placid sky, and the people passing by, and daily our
acquiescence presses down on us from above and we have no room to be.
It is the children's fault as they swarm, for we cannot stop caring.

In a bad time, people, from an outpost of empire I write
bewildered, though on about living. It is to set down a nation's
failure of nerve; I mean complicity, which is signified by the
gaseous stain above us. For a man who
fries the skin of kids with burning jelly is a criminal.
Even though he loves children he is a criminal. Even though his
money pumps your oil he is criminal, and though his programs infest the
    air you breathe he is
criminal and though his honest quislings run your
government he is criminal and though you do not love his enemies he is
criminal and though you lose your job on his say-so he is criminal
and though your country will founder without him he is criminal and
though he has transformed the categories of your refusal by the pressure of
    his media he is a criminal.
And the consenting citizens of a minor and docile colony

are cogs in a useful tool, though in no way
necessary and scarcely
criminal at all, and their leaders are
honourable men, as for example Paul Martin.

In Germany, the civic square in many towns is
hallowed for people. Laid out just so, with
flowers and fountains and during the war you could come and
relax for an hour, catch a parade or just
get away from the interminable racket of the trains, clattering through the
outskirts with their lousy expendable cargo.
Little cafés often, facing the square. Beer and a chance to relax.
And except for the children it's peaceful here
too, under the sun's warm sedation.

The humiliations of imperial necessity
are an old story, though it does not
improve in the telling and no man
believes it of himself.
Why bring up genocide? Why bring up
acquiescence, profiteering? Why bring up, again,
the deft emasculation of a country by the Liberal Party of Canada?
It is not Mr Martin who sprays the poison mist
on the fields of the Vietnamese, not in person, nor fries civilians –
he is no worse a man than the other sellouts of history:
the Britons who went over to the legionaries, sadly for the sake of the
        larger peace;
the tired professors of Freiburg, Berlin; the statesmen at Munich, those
estimable men. And the lovers of peace, the brisk switchers who
told it in Budapest. Doesn't the
service of quiet diplomacy require dirty hands?
(Does the sun in summer pour its warm light into the square
for us to ignore?)

And then if it doesn't work one is finally
on the winning side – though that is
unkind; Mr Martin is an honourable man, as we are all
Canadians, and honourable men.

And this is void: to participate in an
abomination larger than yourself. It is to fashion
other men's napalm and know it, to be a
Canadian safe in the square and watch the children dance and
dance and smell the lissome burning
bodies to be born in
old necessity to breathe polluted air and
come of age in Canada with lies and vertical on earth no
man has drawn a breath that was not lethal to some brother it is
yank and gook and hogtown linked in
guilty genesis it is the sorry mortal
sellout burning kids by proxy acquiescent
still though still denying it is merely to be human.

6

I am one for whom the world is constantly proving too much –
not this nor that, but the continental drift to barbarian
normalcy frightens me, I am constantly
stiffening before my other foot touches the ground and numb in my
stance I hear the country pouring on past me gladly on all sides,
towed and protesting but pelting very fast downhill,
and though I do not decry each gift of technopolis I can see only the bread
        and circuses to come,
and no man will use a mirror to shave, in case he
glimpse himself and abroad there will come obscenity, a senseless
        procession of holy wars,

and we will fashion the napalm for our side, proud of our clean hands.
I can't converse with friends without discussing Rome, this is
bad news and though the upshot is not that I am constantly
riddled with agonies my thing is often worse for I cannot get purchase on life.

7

Among the flaws that mar my sleep I harbour more than wars for I have
      friends and lacerations,
brave men and spritely women,
whose fears dovetail and though often our gentleness for our beloved
is straight and incomparable,
we impose the roles that feed the other's hankering and go on to
savage what we have made, defacing
images, our own, and thus finally
destroy the beloved trapped inside the image.
And the nerve-ends come apart and we spend
long nights separate in the same bed, turning and turning as if
our dreams were real, for there are
few among us who are competent at being, and few who can
let our lovers be.
And some are freed by the breakdown, but many at once will
lapse back into the game, projecting our
monstrous images back outside us again, where we will
deface them again and again destroy the beloved,
and there is never any end to it while we are alive.

Yet some move through these hard necessities
like losers for awhile, until they
reach a kind of ease in their bodies' loving.
The agony hunger fades; they come to a
different rhythm together, around

the kids and their jobs, that allows for a
tentative joy and also for grieving together.

But mostly each man carries his lover's fate
inside him, which he fears as it stirs because if the drinks are strong
or the conversation proceeds just so it will rise up and contemptuously
destroy him, and at last when he meets the other
with his own fate trapped like a bubble inside her body
there is a baleful chemistry which draws them together for love and the kill.
And out of that horror of life
they take on the crippled roles that each has singled the
other to partner, the voluntary betrayal is
consummated and they are confirmed again
in postures of willing defeat, and furious at their own fresh self-abolition
they tear strips off the other who has been their accessory.
And they walk all night in the street for the fate is still in them,
and it is a rash passer who does not see himself on the go half out of his
      mind with the need to fail and be hurt
for these were brave men and subtle women, spritely lovers
who could not love themselves, and it is
hard that we have only
one life for mostly we cannot command the courage outright to exist,
and the months slip by and still we have not started,
and every year attaches itself behind and we have more to drag.

Faced with the onus of living our civilization, here, in this time,
do we also single out leaders because they will
dishonour us, because they will diminish us?
And they act our hearts' desire for always they are
bulldozed by goddam yankees, menaced by slant-eyed gooks and happily
      there is
no hope that we might come to our own and
live, with our claimed selves, at home in the difficult world.

8

I come to the square each time there is nothing and once, made calm again
by the spare vertical glory of right proportions,
watching the wind cut loose as it riffled the clouds on the skyline, framing
    the towers at noon,
catching the newsboys' raucous cry of race in the streets and the war and
    Confederation going,
smelling the air, the interminable stink of production and transport and
caught once more in the square's great hush with the shoppers, hippies,
    brokers, children, old men dozing alone by the pool and waiting,
feeling the pulse in the bodies jostling past me driving to climax and
    dollars and blood,
making my cry here quick and obscure among many in transit – not as a
lyric self in a skin but divided, spinning off many selves to attend each
    mortal yen as it passed me – thinking of
death in the city, of others' and also my own and of many born afterwards,
I saw that we are to live in the calamitous division of the world
with singleness of eye, and there is
nothing I would not give to be made whole.

Hector de Saint-Denys Garneau,
you came this way and made poems out of your body,
out of the palpable void that opened
between the bones of your spine – if you weren't just
making it up, you thought,
and humbled yourself again.
But your friends could only see that you were a genius,
and humiliated by their nonchalance as they strolled through space, as if
they belonged, as if their tickets had been accepted,
you turned back and fingered the precious emptiness, feeling inside you
the small incessant gush of the cardiac lesion.
And often you left the room when the party was

reaching its climax, and you had been foremost in repartee, Garneau,
and fell crouching upstairs in a sweat by the bed, sick with contrition, and
stammered out holy names,
destroyed by what was quick and sexual in Montreal.
But you lasted ten years more, in a suave vertigo
assaying the void with your nerve-ends, watching your
friendships go dead, your poems, nursing
the adorable death of the Son in your own imperious cells, a man made
empty for love of God, straining to be only
an upright will in the desert, until at last the world's hypnotic glitter
was made single, in the grace of renunciation.

But not for us; for the kids, and the calm, and the
endless beckoning things
divide us as they pass by with clowns, the tawdry
yammering goes on inside and it yanks us here and every
whichway, we are on all fronts and forming
new precious attachments and
often they stun us till what is authentic is obliterated and heeding it or
even locating it becomes one more hangup, all that great longing keeps
banging back against the miscellaneous clobber of day to day.

And by these distractions we are saved, for there is a deadly route that the
    blood knows
and the obscure inklings of the implacable imagination declare it,
lonely among bedclothes before the light on Tuesdays;
and though I will not speak of where I have not been it is
the graveyard of many for want of the lore of emptiness,
which once was a sane thing, but now of those who begin
their lonely inward procession
I do not know a chastened handful who survive.

Catatonic exemplar,
cardiac, scrupulous, hagridden – you, Hector,

our one patrician maker, mangled spirit,
you went all out for fame and when you knew you would not survive in the
    world you turned to sainthood,
and you beat down the thought for the pride, you retreated to
Sainte-Catherine, watching your blood lap wide on the lake at sunset,
dreaming of John of the Cross, patron of void, dreaming of Jesus,
and you felt the ferns come muscling up through your body, the brutal
    ferns in spring, it was all
detachment you hoped, it was exquisite
penetration, it was
fear of life, the mark of Canada.
And now across
two decades and two nations, Saint-Denys Garneau, my blessed stricken
original, still haunted by the
space between your ribs, maker and brother and comfortless, my
lone heroic starter: out of my own wrong start, I
keep my distance and praise.

The crowds gust through the square, the crowds and the refuse.
The luminous towers preside.
Of high detachment there are many counterfeits;
the world is itself, though sundry.
And I will not enter void till I come to myself
nor silence the world till I learn its lovely syllables,
the brimful square and the dusk and the war and the crowds in motion at
    evening, waiting to be construed,
for they are fragile, and the tongue must be sure.

9

Here, as I sit and watch, the rusty leaves hang taut with departure.
The last few tourists pose by the Moore and snap their proof that they too
    were alive.
And what if there is no regenerative absence?
What if the void that compels us is only
a mood gone absolute?
We would have to live in the world.
What if the banks of high-rise are nothing but
banks of dreary high-rise, they do not release the spirit by
fraying its attachment,
for the excellent reason that there is nowhere else to go?
We would have to live in it, making our home on earth.
    Or else a man might go on day by day
in love with emptiness, dismayed each time he meets
good friends, fine buildings and grass in the acres of concrete, feeling the
city's erotic tug begin once more, perpetually
splayed alive by the play of his bungled desires;
though some do not salute the death of the body
before they have claimed its life, but crippled they summon
the fury from within, they tilt at
empire, empire, lethal adversary.
But I am one who came to
idolatry, as in a season of God,
taking my right to be from nothingness.

Across the square the crisp leaves blow in gusts, tracing
the wind's indignant lift in corners,
filling the empty pool.
People plod past through the raw air, lost in their overcoats.
I hunch down close to my chest and eat smoke.

And when the void became void I did
let go, though derelict for months
and I was easy, no longer held by its negative presence,
as I was earlier disabused of many things in the world
including Canada, and came to know I still had access to them,
and I promised to honour each one of my country's failures of nerve and its
    sellouts.

To rail and flail at a dying civilization,
to rage in imperial space, condemning
soviet bombers, american bombers – to go on saying
no to history is good.
And yet a man does well to leave that game behind, and go and find
some saner version of integrity,
although he will not reach it where he thinks to, in the
vacant spaces of his mind – they are so
occupied. Better however to try.

For we are not allowed to enter God's heaven, where it is all a
drowsy beatitude, nor is God, the realm above our heads, but
must grow up on earth.
Nor do we have recourse to void.
For void is not a place, nor
negation of a place.
Void is not the high cessation of the lone self's burden,
crowned with the early nostalgias;
nor is it rampant around the corner, endlessly possible.
We enter void when void no longer exists.

And best of all is finding a place to be
in the early years of a better civilization.
For we are a conquered nation; sea to sea we bartered

everything that counts, till we have
nothing to lose but our forebears' will to lose.
Beautiful riddance!
And many will make their choice and eat imperial meat.
But some will come to themselves, for there is
no third way at last and these will
pitch their lives in the ranks of civil resistance, deploying
motherwit and guts – sustained
by bloody-minded reverence among the things which are,
and the long will to be in Canada.

The leaves, although they cling against the
wind, do not resist their time of dying.
And I must learn to live it all again, depart again –
the storm-wracked crossing, the nervous descent, the barren wintry land,
and clearing a life in the place where I belong, re-entry
to bare familiar streets, first sight of coffee mugs,
reconnaissance of trees, of jobs done well or badly,
flashes of workaday people abusing their power,
abusing their lives, hung up, sold out, wrenched out of whack
by the steady brunt of the continental breakdown –
finding a place among the ones who live
on earth somehow, sustained in fits and starts
by the deep ache and presence and sometimes the joy of what is.

Freely out of its dignity, the void must
supplant itself. Like God like the soul it must
surrender its ownness, like eternity it must
re-instil itself in the texture of our being here.
And though we have seen our most precious words
withdraw, like smudges of wind from a widening water-calm,
though they will not be charged with presence again in our lifetime, that is

well, for now we have access to new nouns.
As, city, tower, hunger, body, land.

Earth, you nearest, allow me.
Green of the earth and civil grey:
within me, without me and moment by
moment allow me for to
be here is enough and earth you
strangest, you nearest, be home.

Alligator Pie

Wiggle to the laundromat,
Waggle to the sea;
Skip to Casa Loma
And you can't catch me!

ALLIGATOR PIE

Alligator pie, alligator pie,
If I don't get some I think I'm gonna die.
Give away the green grass, give away the sky,
But don't give away my alligator pie.

Alligator stew, alligator stew,
If I don't get some I don't know what I'll do.
Give away my furry hat, give away my shoe,
But don't give away my alligator stew.

Alligator soup, alligator soup,
If I don't get some I think I'm gonna droop.
Give away my hockey-stick, give away my hoop,
But don't give away my alligator soup.

BEING FIVE

I'm not exactly big,
 And I'm not exactly little,
But being Five is best of all
 Because it's in the middle.

A person likes to ride his bike
 Around the block a lot,
And being Five is big enough
 And being Four is not.

And then he likes to settle down
 And suck his thumb a bit,

And being Five is small enough,
　　But when you're Six, you quit.

I've thought about it in my mind –
　　Being Five, I mean –
And why I like it best of all
　　Is 'cause it's In Between.

SKYSCRAPER

Skyscraper, skyscraper,
Scrape me some sky:
Tickle the sun
While the stars go by.

Tickle the stars
While the sun's climbing high,
Then skyscraper, skyscraper
Scrape me some sky.

KAHSHE OR CHICOUTIMI

If I lived in Temagami,
Temiskaming, Kenagami,
Or Lynx, or Michipicoten Sound,
I wouldn't stir the whole year round

Unless I went to spend the day
At Bawk, or Nottawasaga Bay,
Or Missinabi, Moosonee,
Or Kahshe or Chicoutimi.

WORM

Some people think a worm is rude,
'Cause he's mostly not in a talkative mood.

And other people think he's dumb,
'Cause he likes you to call, but he doesn't come.

But I've got a worm, and his name is Worm,
And he lives in a jar with a bunch of germs,

And Worm is as smart as a worm can be.
I talk to him and he listens to me:

I tell him the time I fell downstairs
And I teach him the names of my teddy bears

And we both sit still, and I hear the things
That you hear when a worm begins to sing –

About dirt in the yard, and tunnels, and drains,
And having a bath in the grass when it rains.

And we plan about snacks, and not washing your hands,
And the letter J. And he understands.

SUZY GREW A MOUSTACHE

Suzy grew a moustache,
    A moustache,
    A moustache,
Suzy grew a moustache,
    And Polly grew a beard.

Suzy looked peculiar,
    Peculiar,
    Peculiar,
Suzy looked peculiar,
    And Polly looked weird.

Suzy got the garden-shears,
    Garden-shears,
    The garden-shears,
Suzy got the garden-shears
    And Polly got a bomb.

Now Suzy's face is smooth again,
    Smooth again,
    Smooth again,
Suzy's face is smooth again,
    And Polly's face is gone.

THE COMING OF TEDDY BEARS

The air is quiet
    Round my bed.
The dark is drowsy
    In my head.

The sky's forgetting
　　To be red,
And soon I'll be asleep.

A half a million
　　Miles away
The silver stars
　　Come out to play,
And comb their hair
　　And that's OK
And soon I'll be asleep.

And teams of fuzzy
　　Teddy bears
Are stumping slowly
　　Up the stairs
To rock me in
　　Their rocking chairs
And soon I'll be asleep.

The night is shining
　　Round my head.
The room is snuggled
　　In my bed.
Tomorrow I'll be
　　Big they said
And soon I'll be asleep.

TRICKING

When they bring me a plate
Full of stuff that I hate,

Like spinach and turnips and guck,
I sit very straight
And I look at the plate
And I quietly say to it: "YUCK!"

Little kids bawl
'Cause I used to be small,
And I threw it all over the tray.
But now I am three
And I'm much more like me –
I yuck till they take it away.

But sometimes my dad
Gets terriffickly mad,
And he says, "Don't you drink from that cup!"
But he can't say it right
'Cause he's not very bright –
So I trick him and drink it all up.

Then he gets up and roars;
He stomps on the floor
And he hollers, "I warn you, don't eat!!"
He counts up to ten
And I trick him again:
I practically finish the meat.

Then I start on the guck
And my daddy goes "Yuck!"
And he scrunches his eyes till they hurt.
So I shovel it in
And he grins a big grin.
And then we have dessert.

WILLIAM LYON MACKENZIE KING

William Lyon Mackenzie King
Sat in the middle & played with string
And he loved his mother like anything –
William Lyon Mackenzie King.

THERE WAS A MAN

There was a man who never was.
This tragedy occurred because
His parents, being none too smart,
Were born two hundred years apart.

DIRTY GEORGIE

Georgie's face was
Never clean,
Georgie smelled like
Gasoline.

Kissing Georgie –
Mighty fine!
Just like kissing
Frankenstein.

Georgie, Georgie,
Wash your face,
Or we'll kick you out
Of the human race:

Not because you're ugly,
Not because you're cute,
Just because your dirty ears
Smell like rubber boots.

INSPECTOR DOGBONE GETS HIS MAN

Inspector Dogbone
    Is my name
And catching bad guys
    Is my game

I catch them hot
    I catch them cold
I catch them when they're
    Nine days old

I catch them here
    I catch them there
I catch them in
    Their underwear

I like to catch them
    By the toes
Or by the moustache
    Or the nose

From Corner Brook
    To Calgary
There's not a cop
    Can copy me

'Cause every time
      I catch a crook
I hang him up
      On a big brass hook –

Yet here I sit
      In the old Don Jail:
Come gather round
      And I'll tell my tale.

One day as I
      Was walking out
I caught a bad guy
      By the snout

He robbed a million-
      Dollar bank
I grabbed his snout
      And gave a yank

I grabbed his snoot
      And gave a flick
But then he played
      A bad-guy trick:

His greasy beak
      Was big and tough –
But with a snap
      He bit it off

And just like that
      His smelly schnozz

Had vanished down
    His smelly jaws!

At once I grabbed him
    By the knee:
He ate that too
    And laughed at me

His neck, his arms,
    His back, his feet –
Whatever I seized
    The man would eat

Till all there was
    Was just a mouth –
Which swallowed itself,
    And scampered south.

The case was gone!
    The case was gone!
The nose and the toes
    And the face were gone!

I had no crook
    I had no crime –
My mighty brain
    Worked overtime

And figured out
    A mighty plan
For Dogbone always
    Gets his man.

Without a crime
    Without a crook
The only person
    Left to book

Was one whom I
    Had long suspected –
Inspector Dogbone,
    Whom I arrested

I didn't quake
    I didn't quail
I threw myself
    In the old Don Jail

And here I sit
    Till the end of time
Easing my soul
    With a Dogbone rhyme,

The victim of
    A bad guy's mouth,
Which swallowed itself
    And scampered south.

But please recall
    As I rot in jail –
Inspector Dogbone
    Didn't fail!

And please remember
    If you can –
Inspector Dogbone
    Got his man!

THINKING IN BED

I'm thinking in bed,
'Cause I can't get out
Till I learn how to think
What I'm thinking about;
What I'm thinking about
Is a person to be –
A sort of a person
Who feels like me.

I might still be Alice,
Excepting I'm not.
And Snoopy is super,
But not when it's hot;
I couldn't be Piglet,
I don't think I'm Pooh,
I know I'm not Daddy
And I can't be you.

My breakfast is waiting.
My clothes are all out,
But *what* was that thing
I was thinking about?
I'll never get up
If I lie here all day;
But I still haven't thought,
So I'll just have to stay.

If I was a Wild Thing
I 'spect I would know.
I might have been Batman,
But I don't think so.

There's so many people
I don't seem to be –
I guess I'll just have to
Get up and be me.

THE DINOSAUR DINNER

Allosaurus, stegosaurus,
Brontosaurus too,
All went off for dinner at the
Dinosaur zoo;

Along came the waiter, called
Tyrannosaurus Rex,
Gobbled up the table
'Cause they wouldn't pay their checks.

THE SPIDER'S WEB

The sun upon a spider's web
       Makes jewels in the air,
As though the light was tangled up
       In someone's windy hair,

Or in a flight of skipping-stones
       Across a river's flare,
Or in a mind of many thoughts,
       Whose owner isn't there.

THE SECRET PLACE

There's a place I go, inside myself,
　　Where nobody else can be,
And none of my friends can tell it's there –
　　Nobody knows but me.

It's hard to explain the way it feels,
　　Or even where I go.
It isn't a place in time or space,
　　But once I'm there, I *know.*

It's tiny, it's shiny, it can't be seen,
　　But it's big as the sky at night ...
I try to explain and it hurts my brain,
　　But once I'm there, it's right.

There's a place I know inside myself,
　　And it's neither big nor small,
And whenever I go, it feels as though
　　I never left at all.

THE FAITHFUL DONUT
　　(*Slowly, with feeding*)

Far across the ocean,
　　Far across the sea,
A faithful jelly donut
　　Is waiting just for me.

Its sugar shines with longing,
　　Its jelly glows with tears;

My donut has been waiting there
    For twenty-seven years.

O faithful jelly donut,
    I beg you don't despair!
My teeth are in Toronto, but
    My heart is with you there.

And I will cross the ocean,
    And I will cross the sea,
And I will crush you to my lips,
    And make you one with me.

THE MUDDY PUDDLE

I am sitting
In the middle
Of a rather Muddy
Puddle,
With my bottom
Full of bubbles
And my rubbers
Full of Mud,

While my jacket
And my sweater
Go on slowly
Getting wetter
As I very
Slowly settle
To the Bottom
Of the Mud.

And I find that
What a person
With a puddle
Round her middle
Thinks of mostly
In the muddle
Is the Muddi-
Ness of Mud.

BUTTERFLY

Butterfly,
    butterfly,
life's a
    dream;

all that we
    see,
and all that we
    seem,

here for a
    jiffy
and then
    goodbye –

butterfly,
    butterfly,
flutter
    on by.

LIZZY'S LION

Lizzy had a lion
    With a big, bad roar,
And she kept him in the bedroom
    By the closet-cupboard door.

Lizzy's lion wasn't friendly,
    Lizzy's lion wasn't tame –
Not unless you learned to call him
    By his Secret Lion Name.

One dark night, a rotten robber
    With a rotten robber mask
Snuck in through the bedroom window –
    And he didn't even ask.

And he brought a bag of candy
    That was icky-sticky-sweet,
Just to make friends with a lion
    (If a lion he should meet).

First he sprinkled candy forward,
    Then he sprinkled candy back;
Then he picked up Lizzy's piggy-bank
    And stuck it in his sack.

But as the rotten robber
    Was preparing to depart,
Good old Lizzy's lion wakened
    With a snuffle and a start.

And he muttered, "Candy? – piffle!"
    And he rumbled, "Candy? – pooh!"

And he gave the rotten robber
An experimental chew.

Then the robber shooed the lion,
Using every name he knew;
But each time he shooed, the lion
Merely took another chew.

It was: "Down, Fido! Leave, Leo!
Shoo, you good old boy!"
But the lion went on munching
With a look of simple joy.

It was: "Stop, Mopsy! Scram, Sambo!
This is a disgrace!"
But the lion went on lunching
With a smile upon his face.

Then old Lizzy heard the rumble,
And old Lizzy heard the fight,
And old Lizzy got her slippers
And turned on the bedroom light.

There was robber on the toy-shelf.
There was robber on the rug.
There was robber in the lion
(Who was looking rather smug).

But old Lizzy wasn't angry,
And old Lizzy wasn't rough.
She simply said the Secret Name:
"Lion – that's enough."

Then old Lizzy and her Lion
    Took the toes & tum & head,
And they put them in the garbage,
    And they both went back to bed.

THE NOTAPOTAMUS

I thought I saw a potamus,
Asleep upon a cotamus,
But when I reached the spotamus,
The potamus was notamus.

It must have got monotamous,
Just sleeping on that cotamus –
So, feeling hot-to-trotamus,
It took off like a shotamus!

O naughty notapotamus,
I liked your style alotamus.
In story, song, and thoughtamus
You're gone, but not forgotamus.

THE WIZARD

I went to see the wizard
In the middle of the night.
His eyes were fierce and far away,
His cloak was burning bright.

"O wizard, can you teach me
How to rise and fly away?"
He stared at me, and glared at me,
And taught me what to say:

"Zoomberry, zoomberry, zoomberry pie:
Zoomberry, zoomberry, now I can fly."

I said it once, I said it twice,
I said it three times three;
With mighty shout I bawled it out
Until he growled at me,

"You have to say it softly,
You have to say it slow,
You have to whisper it at night
As off to sleep you go:

"'Zoomberry, zoomberry, zoomberry pie:
Zoomberry, zoomberry, now I can fly.'"

So home I went, and down I lay,
And closed my sleepy eyes,
And as I whispered "Zoomberry,"
I felt my body rise.

Then up I floated, off I flew,
The whole wide world to see –
And now each night I tell the spell
The wizard taught to me:

"Zoomberry, zoomberry, zoomberry pie:
Zoomberry, zoomberry, now I can fly ..."
(Zoomberry, zoomberry, now I can fly.)

SILVERLY

Silverly,
    Silverly,
Over the
    Trees
The moon drifts
    By on a
Runaway
    Breeze.

Dozily,
    Dozily,
Deep in her
    Bed,
A little girl
    Dreams with the
Moon in her
    Head.

PERCY

Percy was a pixie,
    A pixie of renown,
He played his little pixie pipe
    All around the town.

He played a pixie hornpipe,
    He played a pixie lay,
And people came from miles around
    To hear the pixie play,

For Percy played it roundabout,
    And Percy played it square,
And Percy played the stories
    That were jostling in the air.

Along the streets of Kensington,
    And in the Beaches too,
In Chinatown, and Cabbagetown,
    He played the whole day through,

Until his pixie piping
    Was a glory in the street,
A ticklish hallelujah
    For the music in our feet.

And though his pipe is silent now,
    And though the stories fade,
I still can hear the music
    That the pixie piper played.

THE BRATTY BROTHER

I dumped the bratty brother
In a shark-infested sea;
By dusk the sea was empty, and
The brat was home with me.

I mailed the bratty brother
To a jail in Moosonee;
The sobbing jailer mailed him back
The next day, C.O.D.

I wept, and hurled the bratty
Brother off the CN Tower;
He lolloped through the living room
In less than half an hour.

So now I keep my brother
In the furnace, nice and neat.
I can't wait till December
When my Dad turns on the heat.

DEAD MEN IN EDMONTON

Dead men in Edmonton
Lie very still,
Dead men in Edmonton
Under the hill.

Some by a fever, and
Some by a chill –
Dead men in Edmonton
Lie very still.

(They know a secret, and
One day we will:
Dead men in Edmonton,
Under the hill.)

A WALK IN THE WOODS

We walked in the woods
Where the wild ones stay,
And they didn't show their faces,
But they didn't run away.

It was quiet in the woods,
And the wild ones heard
When we brushed against the bushes,
But they didn't say a word.

Then we waited in the woods,
And we listened to the air;
And they heard us keeping quiet,
And we felt them being there.

MELVIS AND ELVIS

Melvis the monster
And Elvis the elf
Were hunting for books
On the library shelf –

One on the carpet,
And one in a chair,
So neither one knew
That the other was there.

Now, Elvis was hoping
To pick out a story

With pictures of monsters
Both friendly and scary,

While Melvis was learning
To read by herself,
And she thought, "What I need
Is the tale of an elf."

Well they sought and they searched
And they searched and they sought,
They pulled down the books
And they thumbed through the lot,

But hard as they hunted,
And search as they might,
Nothing they looked at
Was totally right.

Then Elvis said, "Phooey!"
And Melvis said, "Bother!"
And with that, they spun round
And they stared at each other.

Said El, "You're a monster."
Said Mel, "You're an elf."
Then they shouted "Hurray!"
And they banged on the shelf –

For each was astonished
At what they could see:
A storybook person
As real as could be,

And each was enchanted,
Because it was clear
The thing they had longed for
Was already here.

Then Elvis taught Melvis
To play hide-and-seek,
And they raced round the room
Till their bladders were weak,

Hiding in secret
(For real or pretend),
And whooping it up
When they found their new friend –

Till at last it was time
For a quieter game,
And Melvis taught Elvis
To spell his own name.

Then Melvis helped Elvis
Reach high on the shelves,
And he pulled down a book about
Monsters and elves,

And tucked in a comer,
Like bears in a den,
They read it, and read it,
And read it again.

GOOFUS

Sometimes my mind is crazy
    Sometimes my mind is dumb
Sometimes it sings like angel wings
    And beeps like kingdom come.

My mother calls me Mary
    My father calls me Fred
My brother calls me Stumblebum
    And kicks me out of bed.

Go tell it on a T-shirt
    Go tell a TV screen:
My summy's turning tummersaults
    And I am turning green.

Don't come to me in April
    Don't come to me in Guelph
Don't come to me in anything
    Except your crummy self.

I haven't got a dollar
    I haven't got a dime
I haven't got a thing to do
    But write these goofy rhymes.

Sometimes my mind is crazy
    Sometimes my mind is dumb
Sometimes it sings like angel wings
    And beeps like kingdom come.

YOU TOO LIE DOWN

Over every elm, the
    half-light hovers.
Down, you lie down too.
Through every shade of dusk, a hush
    impinges. Robins
settle to the nest; beneath, the deep earth
breathes, it
          breathes. You too lie
down, the drowsy room is
close and come to darkness.
            Hush, you
too can sleep at last. You
          too lie down.

The Death
of Harold Ladoo

Harold Sonny Ladoo was born in Trinidad, in 1945 or earlier, of East Indian descent. In 1968 he came to Toronto, where he published two novels with the House of Anansi. He was murdered in 1973 during a visit to Trinidad.

The backyards wait in the dusk. My neighbour's elm
           is down now, dismembered, the chainsaw finally
       muzzled, and the racket of kids has dwindled
to dreams of crying, *Tim-ber!* as it fell.
                   Along the scrubby lane
     the air-conditioners hum, they
           blur small noises.
                   Darkness rises through the leaves.
And here I am, Harold,
       held in the twitchy calm of the neighbourhood, remiss and
               nagged by an old compulsion, come at last
     to wrestle with your death –
               waiting on magisterial words
                 of healing and salute,
         the mighty cadence poets summoned in their grief
             when one they cherished swerved from youth to dead
               and every thing went numb, until
     their potent words resumed his life and I, though
             least of these and unendowed
                     with Muse or Holy Ghost, still
         lug your death inside me and it
             festers still, it
will not be placated till I speak the words of high release,
               which flex and gather now
     as though somehow the fences' silhouette, the
         linden tree, the bulk of the
                 huddled garages – there but
       going fast in the fading light –
all, all have ripened here to ampler elegiac presence,
               and the dusk and the hush and the
         pressure of naked need
begin at last to coax your dying into words of wholeness and salute.

Five years ago this spring –
        remember how we met? We sat drinking
    outside at the Lion, sun lathering us, the transport-trailers
            belting along on Jarvis, your manuscript
        between us on the table and
                what did I see?
A skinny brown man in a suit – voice tense, eyes shifting, absurdly
        respectful ... and none of it connected:
    that raucous, raging thing I'd read, and this
            deferential man.
Then it began: your body
            didn't work   you had to learn it all
    right now!   it was part of one huge saga (*what* was?)
                Greek restaurants
    till 3 A.M. after class, in the cane fields
            till eight and you learned to read
                    in hospitals, the professors here
    all dunces   your vicious unlikely family and
            dead soon, you would be
                    dead and nothing
        came right on the page, you
    pitched the lot   was this guy for real?   then it hit, the
                whirling saga
        the table going away, the
            drinks, the traffic   those liquid
    eyes unhooding, a current like jolts of
            pain in the air – I'd
never seen the need to write so
            badly founded; nor so quiet, deadly, and convincing –
    and I was at home, relaxed.

        How it all floods back in a rush in my forearms:
    those endless sessions together, the
            swagger & hard-edge glee.

And as my nerve-ends flicker now, they do they
            start up in the dark –
    the words I've waited for:
If any be rage,
        pure word, you:
    not in the mouth   not in the brain, nor the blastoff ambition –
            yet pure word still, your
        lit up body of rage. As though ...

But Harold – Harold, what bullshit! sitting here making up epitaphs.
            You're *dead.*
        Your look won't smoulder on Jarvis again, and
            what is hard
is when good men die in their rising prime, and the scumbags flourish,
            and the useless *Why?* that
        flails up cannot furnish even
    the measure of such injustice,
            save by its uselessness.
    And what am I doing, stirring the pot again,
        when every riff I try, every pass at a high salute
                goes spastic in my mouth?...
            And suppose I come closer, come clean –
    what's in it for me?

But the friendship moved so fast; at the Lion, already
we were comrades.
That's how it seemed.
For I was drunk on the steady flood of talent,
the welter of manuscripts that kept
surfacing month after month, and often with lives attached. I'd seen
good sudden friends appear, two dozen savage hacks
descending like a tribe,
a shaggy new
community of rage where each had thought himself alone,

and claimed our heritage, not
by choice but finding it laced from birth through our being:
denial of spirit and flesh,
and strove we hoped to open room to live in, enacting in words
the right to ache, roar, prattle, keen, adore – to be
child, shaggy animal, rapt
celebrant and all in the one skin,
flexing manic selves in the waste of the self's deprival. And I was
flesh at last and alive and I cherished those
taut, half-violent women and men
for their curious gentleness, and also the need
in extremis to be.
They made good books,
and the time was absolute. And often we flirted with chaos
although it was more than that, for mostly I cherished
the ones who wore their incandescent pain
like silent credentials, not flaunting it,
and who moved into their own abyss with a hard, intuitive grace.
And the breakdown quotient was high, but
we did what had to be done and
we were young, Harold and sitting there
on the porch of the Lion in sunlight, drinking beside you,
listening hour after hour,
I saw that you made one more among us, dragging old
generations of pain as perpetual fate and landscape, bound
to work it through in words;
and I relaxed.

          Our talks all blur together. That soft voice pushing
     deep, and deeper, then catching fire – thirty novels, fifty –
          a lifetime of intricate fury, no, four
    centuries of caste and death
         come loose in your life, the murdered
       slaves come loose, great cycles of race and feuds,

all christened with
boots and machetes, the bloodwash of birth and vengeance,
                come loose the wreckage of mothers and sons in
     Trinidad, white
          daytime Christ and the voodoo darkness loose, your voice
               hypnotic and I sat there
          time and again in a dazzle –
then: quick change, the
          swagger of tricky humility – and then again, quick change and
               four days writing straight, no
          sleep say it *all*;
and then the phonecall – one more
          livid book in draft: from the Caribbean to
     Canada,
          the saga piecing together.

Driven, caring, proud: it was
community somehow. And your
dying, Harold your dying
diminished the thing on earth we longed to be, for
rampant with making we recognized
no origin but us ...
     But my mind bangs back as I say that, jerks and
bangs backwards.
Why should I tell it like a poem? Why not speak the truth?
although it cancels
all those images of chiselled desolation,
the transcendental heroes I made up
and fastened to the contours of my friends.
But more & more it's a bore, dragging those
props around, arranging
my friends inside.
Piss on the abyss. And on hard intuitive grace.
We were a tiresome gang of honking egos:

graceless, brawling, greedy, each one in love with
style and his darling career. And visions of liberation
danced in our screwed-up heads, we figured
aping those would somehow make us writers,
cock and a dash of the logos –
oh, and Canada;
but all it's done is make us life-and-blood clichés.
Media fodder. Performing rebels. The works.
Wack-a-doo!
For this I tied my life in knots?

And as for you, Ladoo! – you never missed a trick.
You soaked up love like a sponge, cajoling
hundreds of hours, and bread, and fine-tuned publication,
and then accepted them all with a nice indifference,
as though they were barely enough. You had us taped, you knew white
liberals inside out: how to
guilt us; which buttons to push; how hard; how long.
Three different times, in close-mouthed confidence you spoke of
three horrific childhoods: it was *there* you first
gave blood, now you could use it
to write. And I was
lethally impressed, and only later realised
two of the childhoods had to be somebody else's,
and all those dues you paid were so much literature.
You couldn't tell which one of you was real.
But I can, now: you were
a routine megalomaniac, taking the shortcut
through living men and women to try and make it big.
　　But leave me wallow in no more crap about the Anansi years.
Ladoo, you bastard, goodbye: you bled me dry.
You used me! and though the words are
not what I intended, they rankle but let me get them said:
goodbye, and good riddance.

For eight straight years of crud in public places
                we worked to incite a country to belong to.
        But here, on this leafy street,
    I wince at those hectic unreal selves
            I made up year by year,
    and found I could not shed them when I tried to.
                Though how to be in the world?
        And leaving them behind
            I got here needing
        roots, renewal, dwelling space,
                not knowing how to live
        the plain shape of a day's necessities, nor how to heed
    the funny rhythms generated by
            the woman I love, three kids, a difficult craft
        that takes the measure of my life.
            Intricate rhythms of the commonplace:
                    a friend, a sky, a walk through green ravines –
        and I am at home.
Though not to die here, fat & marooned, like a curled-up
                slug in a dream of the suburbs. But for
        now I am
            here, Ladoo, here like
                    this in the yard and tomorrow,
            and often I
        think of those headlong years with bafflement,
            good friends and deaths ago,
    when voice by voice we raged like a new noise in the orchestra
    as though each deficit we harboured needed only to be named
            to take on public resonance,
and each honest word on a page meant news of another comrade –
        like you, Harold.

        But the books kept
        pouring through your system like heart attacks,

nine in three years,
and the manuscripts rose in your bedroom, uneditable for
new ones came and
sabotaged your life. And
the life and the work wrenched farther apart;
you stabbed a man, berserk they had
doped your drink and you
went on brooding on style, your ear emphatic with
Faulkner, Milton, Achebe,
Naipaul, Gibson, Harris, García Márquez:
these men you meant to
write into the ground.
No Pain Like This Body came out, that spare and
luminous nightmare and you
went back to
dishwashing, writing all night and flexing new
voices, possessed;
each time we met, your body was
closer to skeletal fury,
your eyes more
deadly and on fire.
And I watched bemused, and awed, as the circles grew
tighter and tighter, those frenzied drafts more
brilliant, and botched, and envious.

For I needed you, Harold, as
outlaw, rock-bottom
loser, one more time that
perfect outsider forging his way through sheer raw talent & nerve.
And I cherished that sanctified rage, I believe I
sponged off it.
Me, a nice WASP kid from the suburbs – how could I
live it on my own?
I could barely raise my voice if somebody stepped on my foot in a movie.

But this, now! this had
hair on it. It stank! It breathed like a ten-ton truck.
It bled, and it called for blood.
I wanted some of that.
And not just you: I mean
the whole chaotic gospel.
There was something in me that craved the welter of sudden friendships,
the unpurged intensity, booze, the all-night sessions,
even the breakdowns, the trials & suicides and underneath it all,
half crazed,
the pressure of unremitting talent
revved up and honing in through
marathons of drafts.
It was a power source, it validated words
and the dubious act of writing.
But make no mistake, Ladoo:
I was devouring you too, in the overall
carnage and we did feed off each other,
you gave your blood at last.
I needed you to be the thing of fantasy
I now detest, as also I detest
the shoddy yen in myself.
Jesus! that kindly editor
with his handy thesaurus & verse –
out for the kill, like all the others
taking what he could get: salvation by proxy,
which meant raw energy, and the will to charge ahead
and live in words, and not ask any questions,
no matter who got screwed.
Say it: I used you, Harold,
like a hypocrite voyeur.

The wide night drifts and soars.
From here to the luminous moon, how many

burnt-out rocketships go stranded
in flawless orbit, whirling through the
stations of mechanical decay
in outer space, our dump though once sublime,
the pleasure ground of God while he was Lord?
But they preside up there. And here – down
here is jumble:
version by version I shuffle images of you
and cannot make them fit.
A man should not make of his friends a
blur of aesthetic alternatives;
nor of himself, though it feels good.
Yet I also remember your sideways grin, the way it slid like a slow fuse.
And what was real was not the adrenalin highs,
the hype and ego-baths. Not only that.
Men and women were real, for sometimes
they handled each other gently.
As one spun out in the frenzy of his number
another would be beside him, as if to say,
"I do not take this seriously,
though you must ... Keep pushing. You can be
more than this."
Beneath the pyrotechnics, beneath the endless
bellyful of ego, yes and even though
each one of us kept skittering through
the tyranny dance of his difficult compulsions,
what surfaced day after day was a
deep tough caring.
Quizzical. Easy. Frustrated. For real.
Allowing the clamour & jazz, yet
reaching past them, past
the very act of words,
to the plain gestures of being human together.
    And I honour the books, but now what fastens me

is not the books but the lives.
And my heart spins out to hold each one, to
cherish them entire, although
I could not say that face to face and finally
too little has come real for me, in the
casual blurt of day to day
the roots and resonance I crave too seldom cohere,
and it is only here that daily living half makes sense at all,
and I cannot relinquish a single one of those whose lives went
blundering through to love, albeit
ropily, and grew indelible.
And I unsay nothing, friend I must continue
locked with you for keeps in this tug of cherishing war,
but always now I return to the deep, unscheduled ground of caring
in which we lived our lives,
and the words arrive.

> Great raging maker, Ladoo: go dead and legendary
>   in permanent regions of praise.
> If any be end, or
>   comely by excess of being;
>   if any be incandescent,
>   on earth like me and gone ...

But still it is not enough.
I know words too, but when I hear your inflections on the
subway now I
turn and always you are dead;
nothing but dead.
What more is there to say?
I would rather spit on your grave than decorate this poem with your death.

> And yet to
>   die, Harold,

that's hard. To die –
                    simply to die, and
            not to be:
            no more to
        saunter by on the sidewalk, the
            way a human does,
        sensing the prick of
                    renewal each spring
in small green leaves and also the used-up bodies of
        winos, for these come
                    mildly rife once more.
        To be finished.
Commotion between the legs: no more to
                    accede to its
                blurred supremacy, the way a
                    human does.
            Nor to
        spend your last good
    muscle or wit on something you
            half believe in, half
        despise. Not even to know
                the wet sweet tangled
        stink of earth after rain;
                    a streetcar's
        clatter; the grain of wood
                in a desk the way
        a human does. And not to feel
                exasperated pleasure any longer
as flesh you instigated shoulders
                    pell-mell past you, out to
        live it all from the start. It's hard,
            I cannot imagine –
                    to be under ground.
        And the press of another life on your own, no

                    miracle but acts &
        patience that cohere: all that
                    sweet & cross-hatched bitter noble aching sold-out
        thrash of life, all
                gone as you reached it, Harold I cannot
                    imagine, to be
                        dead the way to be
            not a
                    human does.

                                I I

One drowsy bird, from another yard, and again
the neighbourhood is still,
the linden tree, the fence, the huddled garages, gone
anonymous in the dark. And though we
make our peace as man and man
the words haven't come to praise you – oh but friend,
you should not have gone to the island alone,
you should not be dead so soon!
    But I'm floundering still, and every cell in my body
bridles, and tells me this is only beginning;
and I must brood against the grain again,
taking the long way round, interrogating
more than just the accident of who you were.
For often at night
when the stillness begins to
tick, or if I take on too many meetings,
there is a question, not my own, which stymies my life:
"What good are poets in a time of dearth?"
Hölderlin asked that, master of poets. Who knew.
But I just get embarrassed.
Alienation and Integration: The Role of the Artist in Modern Society.
And mostly I believe the artists further

the systematic murder of the real, and if their work does have
the tang of authentic life
it is one more sign that they are in business to kill.
For a civilization cannot sustain
lobotomy, meaning the loss of awe,
the numbing of *tremendum* – and its holy of holies
goes dead, even the
nearest things on earth
shrink down and lose their savour –
it cannot dispel the numinous, as we have done for
centuries without those exiled gods and demons rushing back
in subterranean concourse,
altered, mocking, bent on genocide.
    For the gods are not dead; they stalk among us, grown murderous.
Gone from the kingdom of reason, they surface
in hellish politics, in towering minds
entranced by pure technique, and in an art refined by
carnage and impotence, where only form is real.
And thus we re-enact
the fierce irrational presencing we denied them – only warped,
grown monstrous in our lives.

A world that denies
the gods, the gods
make mad. And they choose their
instruments with care.
Leaders, artists, rock stars are among their darlings. And
to the artist they promise
redemptive lunacy, and they do bestow the gift but what they deliver
is sauce for the nerve ends, bush-league paranoia,
fame as a usable freak, depression, and silence.
    Yet nothing is wasted. The artist they favour
becomes a priest indeed, he mediates
the sacraments of limbo.

For a world without numinous being is
intolerable, and it is his special vocation
to bludgeon the corpse for signs of life, achieving
impossible feats of resuscitation, returning, pronouncing it
dead again. Opening new
fever paths in the death heaps of a civilization.
And he names the disease, again and again he makes great
art of it, squandering
what little heritage of health and meaning remains,
although his diagnoses are true, they are
truly part of the disease
and they worsen it, leaving
less of life than they found; yet in our time
an art that does not go that route
is deaf and blind, a coward's pastorale,
unless there be grace in words.

But the role comes down like lucid
catharsis: *creator!* taking the poor old
world as neuter space, as one more specimen, sanctioning
mania and rage, the gift of the mutant gods.
And the floating role is alive on its own and always
there now, it idles about & waits, it is after
a man – who knows? bank-clerk, dishwasher, writer, professor –
and when he appears, he is shanghaied.
So, Harold, your ramshackle life
was yanked into orbit, and kindled, and given coherence,
and blasted apart by the play of that living myth.
Almost you had no say.

Galvanic art! new carnal assertions! fresh nervous systems!
            adrenalin ascensions for the chosen!
It is the need to be
            one, to be taken whole & alive

by that which is more than oneself, sensing
the body, the
brain, the being
absolved at last in a radiant therapy, resolved
in single, emphatic wholeness:
to live on fire in words, heroic
betrayal.
And I think of others we knew, comrades in Toronto
who toppled headlong like you to the calm of their own myth,
accepting its violent poise like the fit of a new skeleton, all that
great fury focused now in its settled gestures of being,
their lives in shambles still but redeemed by mythic contours
and it moves like fluid skin around them,
holding the
breakable ego, titanic
energies in place at last, no more
questions – or so it seems to one
with myths galore but no fixed will to inhabit them.
And our lives were single then, we were made
valid, though wasted, for I
know the thing I write and I would
gladly go back to that, gladly but
I do not believe in it.
But you, Harold: you
went and lived in words.
You pushed it past the limit, further than any of us
and also you died of it,
face down, no teeth in your head, at twenty-eight,
dead on a backroad in Trinidad.
Though that I believe in. But not
the vanishing into words.

The night winds come and go
and linden drifts like snow around me:

paradise row, and somehow it is
permitted to live here.
But though things fit themselves now, graciously
easing into place and
are, as
though they had always known,
that too has its proper measure, and cannot stay on
beyond its own good time.
Yet in this blessed breathing space, I see that
every thing must serve too many selves.
And we, who thought by words to blitz
the carnal monuments of an old repression –
we were ourselves in hock, and acting out
possessive nightmares of a
straitened century.
Surprise! we weren't
God's hitmen, nor the
harbingers of raunchy absolutes; and nor is
any thing on earth.
For madness, violence, chaos, all that primitive hankering
was real necessity, yet
bound to the gods' revenge and to
prolong it would be death.

People, people I speak from
private space but all these
civil words keep coming and they
muddle me.
Salvations come & go, they
singe us by the root-hair – to live for
revolution, for the dear one, for chemical highlights
for power for objects for art –
and each one turns demonic, for it too gets cherished as
absolute.

Even that glorious dream
of opening space to dwell in, of speaking the
                    first words of our space –
that too was false, for we cannot
idolize a thing without it going infernal,
            and in this season of dearth
                    there are only idols.
        Though how to live from that and still
    resist real evil, how to keep from
                    quietist fadeouts, that I
        scarcely know. But
epiphanies will come
        as they will come, will
                go; they are not
        trademarks of grace; they
            do not matter, surprise.
"Everything matters, and
                    nothing matters."
    It is harder to live by that on earth and stubborn than to
        rise, full-fledged and abstract,
                    and snag apocalypse.

Harold, how shall I exorcize you?
        This is not for blame.
                    I know that
            it lived *you*, there was no
    choice; some men do carry this century
            malignant in their cells from birth
        like the tick of genetic stigmata,
    and it is no longer
                whether it brings them down, but only
        when. You were a fresh explosion
of that lethal paradigm: the
                    Tragic Artist, *yippee* and

forgive me friend.
But you heard your own death singing, that much I know.
    And went to meet it mesmerized – to get
        the man that got your mother, yes, but also plain
          wooing it, telling Peter you'd
never be back alive. The jet's trajectory
    a long sweet arc of dying, all the way down.
And whatever the lurid scuffle that
    ended the thing – your body
        jack-knifed, pitch dark, in the dirt –
it was after the fact; you had
    lived that moment for years, you were
        already one of the chosen.
    Your final legacy
two minor early novels, one being nearly first-rate.

I read these words and flinch, for I had not meant
to quarrel with you, Harold.
Nor with friends, good men and women, who also lived these things.
Nor with myself.
Though I feel nothing for you
I did not feel before your death,
I loved you, and I owed you words of my own.
But speaking the words out loud has brought me close to the bone.

Night inches through. It's cold. I wish I were sleeping,
or stronger, more rooted in something real
this endless night of the solstice, June, 1975.
Ten minutes more, then bed.
But I know one thing, though
barely how to live it.
We must withstand the gods awhile, the mutants.
And mostly the bearers of gifts, for they have
singled us out for unclean work; and supremely

those who give power, whether at words or
the world for it will bring
criminal prowess.
But to live with a measure, resisting their terrible inroads:
I hope this is enough.
And, to let the beings be.
And also to honour the gods in their former selves,
albeit obscurely, at a distance, unable
to speak the older tongue; and to wait
till their fury is spent and they call on us again
for passionate awe in our lives, and a high clean style.

The Cat
and the Wizard

THE CAT AND THE WIZARD

I

A senior wizard
Of high degree
With a special diploma
In wizardry
Is trudging along
At the top of the street
With a scowl on his face
And a pain in his feet.

A beard, a bundle,
A right-angle stoop,
And a cutaway coat
Embroidered with soup,
A halo of smoke
And a sputtery sound –
The only real magic
Magician around.

> But nobody nowadays
> Welcomes a wizard:
> They'll take in a spaniel,
> Make room for a lizard –
> But show them a conjurer
> Still on the ball,
> And nobody wants him
> Or needs him at all.

His bundle is bulging
With rabbits and string,

And a sort of machine
That he's teaching to sing,
And a clock, and a monkey
That stands on its head,
And a mixture for turning
Pure gold into lead.

He carries a bird's nest
That came from the Ark;
He knows how to tickle
A fish in the dark;
He can count up by tens
To a million and three –
But he can't find a home
For his wizardry.

For *nobody*, nowadays,
Welcomes a wizard;
They'll drool at a goldfish,
Repaint for a lizard,
But show them a magus
Who knows his stuff –
They can't slam their latches down
Quickly enough!

II

In Casa Loma
Lives a cat
With a jet-black coat
And a tall silk hat.
And every day
At half past four

She sets the table
For twelve or more.

The spoons parade
Beside each plate;
She pours the wine,
She serves the steak,
And Shreddies, and turnips,
And beer in a dish –
Though all she can stomach
Is cold tuna fish.

But a cat is a cat
In a castle or no,
And people are people
Wherever you go.

Then she paces about
In the big dining hall,
Waiting and waiting
For someone to call
Who won't be too snooty
For dinner and chat
At the home of a highly
Hospitable cat.

And every evening
At half past eight,
She throws out the dinner
And locks the gate.
And every night,
At half past ten,
She climbs up to bed
By herself, again.

For a cat is a cat
In a castle or no,
And people are people
Wherever you go.

III

One day they meet
In a laundromat,
The lonesome wizard,
The jet-black cat.

And chatting away
In the clammy air,
They find they both like
Solitaire,

And merry-go-rounds,
And candle-light,
And spooky yarns
That turn out right.

They stroll together
Chatting still
To Casa Loma
On the hill

And there the cat
Invites her friend
To share a bite,
If he'll condescend;

And yes, the wizard
Thinks he might –

But just for a jiffy
And one quick bite.

An hour goes by
Like a silver skate.
The wizard moves
From plate to plate.

Two hours go by
Like shooting stars.
The cat produces
Big cigars,

And there in the darkening
Room they sit,
A cat and a wizard,
Candle-lit.

At last the wizard
Takes the pack
From his creaking, reeking,
Rickety back.

He sets it down
With a little shrug,
And pulls a rabbit
From under the rug,

And before you can blink
He's clapping his hands,
And there in the doorway
A peacock stands!

Now he's setting the monkey
Upon its head,
He's turning the silverware
Into lead,

And counting by tens
From a hundred to four
And making a waterfall
Start from the floor

And juggling a turnip,
A plate and a dish,
And turning them all
Into fresh tuna fish.

The cat is ecstatic!
She chortles, she sails
From the roof to the floor
On the banister rails,

And soon the whole castle
Is whizzing with things:
With sparklers and flautists
And butterflies' wings,

And all through the night
The party goes on –
Till it stops in a trice
At the crack of dawn,

And the wizard installs
His pack in a drawer,
While the cat tidies up
The living-room floor.

And as the sky
Is growing red,
They tiptoe up
The stairs to bed.

The wizard's snore
Is rather weird;
The cat is snuggled
In his beard –

Dreaming of tuna fish
End to end,
And rabbits, and having
A brand-new friend.

≈

Perhaps you wonder
How I know
A cat and a wizard
Can carry on so?

Well: if some day
You chance to light
On Casa Loma
Late at night,

Go up to the window,
Peek inside,
And then you'll see
I haven't lied.

For round & round
The rabbits dance,

The moon is high
And they don't wear pants;

The tuna fish
Patrol the hall,
The butterflies swim
In the waterfall,

And high and low
With a hullabaloo
The castle whirls
Like a tipsy zoo!

And in the corner,
If you peer,
Two other figures
May appear.

One is dressed
In a tall silk hat:
The queen of the castle,
The jet-black cat.

The other's a wizard
Of high degree.
The wizard is grinning.
The wizard is me.

HIGH BLUE MEADOWS

When I could fly,
I'd sometimes pass
The morning couched
In meadow grass.

I'd track the ants,
Manoeuvring
To jockey home
A beetle's wing,

Or watch the way
A spider slung
Its innards out
And blithely hung –

And never spend
A thought upon
The high blue meadows
Where I'd gone.

But now the flying
Days are done,
I stake my time
To reach the sun.

The traffic and
The traffic glare
Bring back old
Arabesques of air;

That dip and swoop,
That memory trace
Still animate
This barren place

Where people scotch
Their lives for pay,
And I must serve
A desk all day –

And in my mind
I swivel high,
To claim the time
When I could fly.

1838

The Compact sat in Parliament
To legalize their fun.
And now they're hanging Sammy Lount
And Peter Matthews' son.
And if they catch Mackenzie
They will string him in the rain.
And England will erase us if
Mackenzie comes again.

The Bishop has a paper
That says he owns our land.
The Bishop has a Bible too
That says our souls are damned.
Mackenzie had a printing press.
It's soaking in the bay.

And who will spike the Bishop till
Mackenzie comes again?

The British want the country
For the Empire and the view.
The Yankees want the country for
A yankee barbecue.
The Compact want the country
For their merrie green domain.
They'll all play finders-keepers till
Mackenzie comes again.

Mackenzie was a crazy man.
He wore his wig askew.
He donned three bulky overcoats
In case the bullets flew.
Mackenzie talked of fighting
While the fight went down the drain.
But who will speak for Canada?
Mackenzie, come again!

WHEN I WENT UP TO ROSEDALE

When I went up to Rosedale
I thought of kingdom come
Persistent in the city
Like a totem in a slum.

The ladies off across the lawns
Revolved like haughty birds.
They made an antique metaphor.
I didn't know the words.

Patrician diocese! the streets
Beguiled me as I went
Until the Tory founders seemed
Immortal government –

For how could mediocrities
Have fashioned such repose?
And yet those men were pygmies,
As any schoolboy knows.

For Head reduced the rule of law
To frippery and push.
Tradition-conscious Pellatt built
A folly in the bush.

And Bishop Strachan gave witness,
By the death behind his eyes,
That all he knew of Eden
Was the property franchise.

And those were our conservatives –
A claque of little men
Who took the worst from history
And made it worse again.

The dream of Tory origins
Is full of lies and blanks,
Though what remains when it is gone,
To prove that we're not Yanks?

Nothing but the elegant
For Sale signs on the lawn,
And roads that wind their stately way
To dead ends, and are gone.

When I came down from Rosedale
I could not school my mind
To the manic streets before me
Nor the courtly ones behind.

THE ANT AND THE ELEPHANT

An elephant of noble stance
And philosophic countenance
Lay stricken, smitten to the core,
Beside his open door.

"Alack!" he sobbed, "at last I see
A home is but a mockery.
And therefore I, despite this pain,
Shall never speak again."

Just then a brisk and busy ant
Came by to meet the elephant.
"What's up?" she asked, and turned to where
His trunk distressed the air.

"You ask me why no hope can cheer
The horrid hurt that haunts me here? –
The doors of yore prevail no more!"
The portly Plato swore.

Indeed, the door had come askew;
The lower hinge would not hang true
Because the bolt had fallen out,
Which splayed the door about.

And now the large philosopher
Unfurled a sort of verbal blur.
"My empty home is occupied –
By homelessness," he cried.

The kindly insect (who was not
Conversant with the higher thought)
Had meanwhile spied the bolt, which lay
An inch or two away;

And with a will she shouldered it,
Although her thorax nearly split.
"... Thus dwelling dies, and doom descends;
Authentic language ends."

Then up the frame she lugged the thing
With puffs and pants and pummelling,
Until she braced it half an inch
Above the errant hinge.

"... For what's a house without a door?
The word falls dumb forevermore!
And what is Truth, and what is Love,
When language cannot speak thereof?"

Then, while he stroked his intellect,
She heaved the mighty door erect
And somehow managed to cajole
The bolt to fit the hole.

"... For language is the deepest mode
Of all our being-in-abode;
Therefore in silence must I roam –
A mute without a home."

But as the metal found its place,
Her feelers stuck in the narrow space;
The bolt shot home – and in she went,
A jellied accident.

This roused our hero from his pain,
And, since the door was plumb again,
He stepped inside to catch his breath
And explicate her death.

And there, with pachydermic wail,
He voiced the moral of our tale:
"*One ant, through foolish haste, may fail,
But Truth and Love shall long prevail.*"

SPADINA

Sparrows sniffed the air, and hung
Like hummingbirds with bubble gum
Doing pushups in the sun
    The day we stopped Spadina.

The people paused to touch the air
And breathe the green renewal there
As though the headline was a prayer
    The day we stopped Spadina.

And parking lots came out to play
Arrayed in green instead of grey
And I said, Why not stay this way?
    The day we stopped Spadina.

I watched a woman's face which glowed
I saw computer cards explode
And I heard grass grow on Walmer Road
    The day we stopped Spadina.

And Bishop Strachan from underground
Was half converted by the sound
Of pleasure in Toronto town
    The one and only day we stopped Spadina.

SPRING SONG

The April leaves
    Are restless now,
Electric green
    Along the bough.

They muss the branch
    And mist the air
Like smoky fronds
    Of maidenhair

And itch the april
    Lovers feel –
That quicker spring,
    That deeper real –

Until our wingy
    Nerve-ends strum
Hosannas in
    Delirium,

While saplings set
　　Their borders by
To strut some green
　　Against the sky

And all the vernal
　　Gunga-din
Escorts a carnal
　　Summer in ...

But when October
　　Comes and goes,
And frost and longing
　　Snuff the rose,

Will April leaves
　　Still linger, taut?
Or else be gone,
　　And then be not?

FORTY MERMAIDS

If I were swimming
In the sea
And forty mermaids
Came to me

And every mermaid
Wore a sign
Inviting me
To come and dine

With ocean heroes
Steeped in fame,
Like Captain Kidd
And What's-his-name,

And if the banquet
Hall were spread
With deep-sea ale
And ocean bread

And all the plates
Were living shells
That floated by
On tidal swells

And waiters wore
Their fin and tails
And served us each
A pinch of snails

And then dessert
Arrived in bubbles
And everyone
Was having doubles,

I think I'd stay
An hour or two;
And then I'd swim
Back home to you.

ME AND MY LOVE AND ME

My love is like a waterfall
    That walks the second mile,
But only thee canst turn the key
    To light its sunny smile.

My love is like a Jersey cow
    That nestles in my heart,
But only you canst make it moo
    When Cupid's call doth start.

For love is like the burning sand
    That babbles o'er the lea,
And love is like an ampersand
    That links my love & me,

And love is like a birthday suit
    That wanders high and low,
But how to loot its lovely fruit
    My love shall never know.

A CAUTIONARY VERSE

My child, do not exaggerate,
Lest you provoke a horrid fate –
As ancient oracles relate
And modern texts corroborate.
For if you ever overstate,
Dissimulate, prevaricate,
Or one small midget fact inflate,

The fist of doom will squash you straight.
Suppose, upon a certain date,
Your bus draws near at speed sedate
Till, galled by the thirty-second wait,
You claim it came *two minutes* late!
Before this whopper can abate
Your heart will start to palpitate,
Your vital fluids desiccate,
Your kidneys cease to operate.
Not only that: at lightning rate
Your mental functions, small and great,
Will shrivel and deteriorate
To pablum in your puny pate.
Thereafter, sentiments of hate
Will soon begin to agitate
Your worthy colleagues, man and mate,
And prompt them to retaliate –
Till through the world, a weary weight
Upon the modern welfare state,
You reel, you sob, you slump, you prate,
And choose your life to terminate ...
But let me not too long dilate
Upon the horrors that await
A dastard who, defying fate,
Should ever *once* exaggerate.

SUZIE SAW THE BLUE BALLOON

Suzie saw the blue balloon –
And that was that was *that*;
A funny tug of otherness
Began in no time flat.

The blue balloon was soaring free
From someone's broken string,
And Suzie watched her heart go high
And felt her body sing.

It sang of ladies long ago
In tales her parents told,
It sang of setting out to sea
To find the pot of gold,

It sang a pang of leaving, and an
Ache in all things near,
It sang, goodbye to innocence
In Suzie's now and here.

And things awoke inside her
Which they'd never told her of;
But four years old is not too young
For missing what you love.

Then up the blue balloon revolved
Beyond the maple trees
Till, gaining speed, it disappeared
Like pollen on a breeze,

And Suzie cried her eyes out, while
The kids and grown-ups smiled
(Except her baffled parents, who had
Raised the stricken child).

THE COAT

I patched my coat with sunlight.
It lasted for a day.
I patched my coat with moonlight,
But the lining came away.
I patched my coat with lightning
And it flew off in the storm.
I patched my coat with darkness;
That coat has kept me warm.

SUMMER SONG

The light was free and easy then,
Among the maple trees,
And music drifted over
From the neighbours' balconies;
Half my mind was nodding
With the asters in their ranks,
And half was full to bursting
With a hungry kind of thanks.

It wasn't just the mottled play
Of light along the lawn.
I didn't hope to live back all the
Good times that were gone;
All I wanted was to let
The light and maples be,
Yet something came together as they
Entered into me.

And what was singing in my mind
Was in my body too:
Sun and lawn and aster beds
Murmuring, I do –
Earth, belovèd, yes, I do I
Too am here by grace,
As real as any buried stone
Or any blade of grass.

Breath and death and pestilence
Were not revoked by that.
Heavy things went on, among
The calm magnificat.
Yet as I sat, my body spoke
The words of my return:
There is a joy of being, which you
Must be still and learn.

ODYSSEUS AND TUMBLEWEED

Odysseus and tumbleweed
And Paddle-to-the-Sea –
All the famous wanderers,
Calling out to me.

Come away, and come away,
And come away with us,
Harbingers and heroes, on
The journey perilous.

Here I sit and sign my name
To endless paper chains –
Odysseus and tumbleweed
Still chafe within my veins.

Come away, and come away,
And come away at last;
How should you be shacking up
With comfort and the past?

Canada is burning, and I
Could not tell you how –
But Paddle-to-the-Sea is sailing
Wide, and leaving now.

Come away, and come away,
And come away alone;
Follow to the living source
Before you turn to stone.

Here-and-now is real, and I am
Pregnant with the yen,
Yet heroes of the distance draw me
Out beyond my ken:

Odysseus and tumbleweed
And Paddle-to-the-Sea –
All the famous wanderers,
Calling out to me.

NICHOLAS KNOCK

I

Nicholas Knock was a venturesome boy.
     He lived at Number Eight.
He went for walks in the universe
     And generally got home late.

But Nicholas Knock was always around
     When the ice-cream truck went *ching*.
He dug up flowers, to watch them grow,
     And he mended them with string.

He found a chipmunk, shivering like a
     Fur-cube in the snow.
He nursed it through to the end of March
     And then he let it go.

Acres of grass and acres of air –
     Acres of acres everywhere:
The sun shone high, and the moon shone low
     And Nicholas didn't care.

So Nicholas Knock went doodling
     Through summer & winter & spring.
His mind had funny edges
     And the ice-cream truck went *ching*.

II

One year it was Tuesday; Nicholas Knock
Went noodling off for a bit of a walk.
He hid on his brother; he raced a dog;

He helped a little kid catch a frog.
Then at the curb, and walking east,
He spied the silver honkabeest.

A trick, a flicker of the light:
The tiny creature, like a flight
Of warblers, seemed to ride the air
And shed a frisky lustre there.
And yet it did not move a hair.

Its eyes were dusky, deep, and clear.
It rose; it flew; it settled near
And Nicholas stood by its delicate side,
Nicholas stood and almost cried.

He left it then, but all that night
He dreamed of its radiant arc in flight.
And when he returned in the morning, the air
Was dimpled with light and the creature was there!
And every day, for a month at least,
He met the silver honkabeest.

III

"O mother, dear mother
        Prepare us a feast;
I'm friends with the silver
        Honkabeest!

"Oh father come quickly,
        I want you to see
For it's shiny and gentle as
        Gentle can be."

"Nicholas Knock!"
    His parents hissed,
"That honkabeast
    Does not exist!"

But Nicholas whinnied,
    And Nicholas sang,
And Nicholas hopped
    Till his bell-bottoms rang.

"I've seen it! I've seen it!
    I'm practically sure!
We meet every morning
    At Brunswick and Bloor."

His parents sat down,
    Exchanging a glance –
Alas for their son
    With his weirdo dance.

Even the neighbours
    Were starting to talk:
What was the matter
    With Nicholas Knock?

His mother declared,
    "I wish I was dead!"
And all in a fury
    His father said,

"This neighbourhood
    Should be policed
To get that vicious
    Honkabeast!"

But Nicholas figured
    Their tempers would mend,
So Nicholas tore off
    To visit his friend.

IV

"Frisky, most silver, serene –
bright step at the margins of air, you
tiny colossus and
winsome and
master me, easy in sunlight, you
gracious one come to me, live in
my life."

V

Well —

They took him to
    A specialist
Who soon prescribed
    An oculist
And then a child
    Psychologist
And last a demon-
    Ologist,
Who knew about
    Astrology
And dabbled in
    Phrenology.

Their diagnoses
    Disagreed,

But on one thing
        They all agreed:
If Nicholas Knock's
        Delusion ceased
(He thought he saw
        A honkabeast),
The boy would mend
        Within a year;
But otherwise
        His fate was clear –

A life in hospitals,
        Designed
To pacify
        The deviant mind,
A life in
        Institutions, meant
To exorcize
        Such devilment;
But still the boy
        Could be released
If he gave up
        His "honkabeast."

Yet heartless, witless,
        Stubborn and slow,
Nicholas Knock
        Kept murmuring, "No."
They yelled at him,
        They shed real tears
Till Nicholas finally
        Plugged his ears;
The more they told him,
        "Kill it dead!"

The harder Nicholas
  Shook his head.

At last they cried,
  "His time is short:
Take him away, to
  Supreme Court!"

VI

Snort! went the
Court clerk, and
Pounded on the table-top.
"Stand!" cried the
Bailiff with a steely-eyed stare.
"Name?" shrilled the
Registrar, and
Poked him with a fountain-pen.
"Swear!" boomed the
Justice with a glare.

"P-please," stammered
Nicholas, "I've seen the silver
Honkabeest –"
"Silence!" roared His
Lordship, "That's a rumour and a lie!
Poppycock and insolence! The
Honkabeast is not a beast –
How are we to know it's not a
Pervert, or a spy?
Eh?
It's probably a pervert *and* a spy.

"Unless you sign a declaration
That the Honkabeast is fiction,
Then I must – as a precaution,
To preserve Confederation –
Place a legal limitation
On your circumambulation
With a minor operation
Which we call decapitation."

Nicholas stood,
He quivered with fear
As he uttered the words
Which I set down here:

"I'm frightened of burglars,
I shake in the dark,
And I'm scared of your sharp sharp knife;
But I love the silver
Honkabeest
More than I love my life.

"I will not sign your paper.
I will not sign your bill.
I've seen him every day for a month
And I hope I always will."

VII

The registrar spoke
    With a dry little cough.
"The lad," she observed,
    "Simply won't be put off;
Perhaps we should listen,
    And not merely scoff."

But His Lordship was raging,
　　He pounded and said,
"Take out the rascal and
　　Chop off his head! –
And by midnight tonight
　　There'll be two of them dead!

"For the army, the navy,
　　The Mounted Police,
The bailiff, the sheriff,
　　And I
Will personally go
　　To the Honkabeast's den,
Preparing to do
　　Or to die.

"With thousands of soldiers,
　　And bombs in each hand,
With missiles and
　　Submarines –
To safeguard our children
　　We'll blast it and blitz it
To billions of
　　Smithereens!

"And at last this land
　　Will be released
From the reign of the terrible
　　Honkabeast!"

VIII

Now Nicholas Knock was a logical boy,
    His powers of thought were good,
But sad to relate, a legal debate
    Was more than he understood.

His head was all cluttered with *right* and *wrong*,
    And *things you mustn't do;*
His mind was all muddled with *evil* and *good*,
    And *"Lies are never true."*

So he stood like a stick, and his eyes looked sick,
    Till he uttered a piercing cry:
"The honkabeest isn't fiction –
    And the honkabeest won't die!"

Then —

Thump! went his
Fist upon the
Forehead of the clerk of court –
Crack! went his shoes against the
Sheriff's bony shin –
Squelch! as his head hit
The bailiff's bulgy stomach, and –
Crrunch! as he caved His Lordship's
Hearing-aid in.

    Then Nicholas whizzed
    And Nicholas whanged
    And Nicholas knocked
    Till their craniums rang.

He covered them in legal briefs,
    He threw them on the floor,
He rolled them up in carpet from
    The courthouse corridor.
He hung them from the curtain rods,
    He coated them in foam,
And told them, gently, "Leave the silver
    Honkabeest alone."
And then he pulled the ceiling down
    And made his way back home.

IX

The sky was as blue as a clear blue sky,
    The sun was hot and high,
When Nicholas came with a flick in his step
    And a fidgety glint in his eye.

The city hung around him, like a
    Quick and dirty scrawl:
The traffic lights, the neon lights,
    And the Bank of Montreal.

He never looked to left or right;
    He came home straightaway
To where the silver honkabeest
    Had met him every day.

He watched the stores; he watched the cars;
    He spied a silver light
That winked at him, and blinked at him –
    And disappeared from sight.

And hunting round to find the thing
    He thought he heard a hoof
That clickered like a honkabeest's,
    But vanished without proof.

And here a snort, and there a tail,
    And silver without end:
He spent a day and night that way,
    But he couldn't find his friend.

But neither could he give it up
    (And this is what was queer),
For every time he started to,
    The thing would reappear

And light would flicker, light would fizz
    Like whispers made of steel,
Till, silver in its secret life,
    The city felt like real.

And if you take a walk on Bloor
    You still can see a boy
Whose face is sometimes in despair
    And sometimes full of joy.

You'll see him stalk and whirl around
    A hundred times at least.
Don't bother him! He's hunting for
    A silver honkabeest.

X

Frisky, most silver, serene —
bright step at the margins of air, you
tiny colossus and
winsome and
master me, easy in sunlight, you
gracious one come to me, live in
my life.

"I didn't write this poem by myself."

Translations from George Faludy

MOROCCO

Yesterday I brought home carrots;
today they are ochre paint.
I watch the skin of thirty-year-old women
parch, and then the hairline cracks begin.
Before my eyes, in random vehement bursts
all things in Marrakesh go hurtling
toward the abrupt perfection of their own deaths.
The strict and cool geometry of night
welters and sags in the torture pit of the sun,
which sows and harvests rot.
All day I draw it deep inside my lungs,
intoxicating spice, and zigzag through the streets,
where every corner is sacred to offhand murder.
Death swarms here.
And if you're young, you're his special darling:
he enters the bed at climax,
hc takes the next chair at meals.

Yet everything I used to love at home
is altered here, become so much
irrelevant window-dressing. Boring. Fake.
And what, back there, disgusted me – this
vicious, barbarous country –
is more like final truth.

I didn't write this poem by myself.
I'm sitting very still. It pleases me
to feel the way my muse, the fear of death,
has peeled me, layer by layer, to the bone.

ON THE TOWER OF THE KASBAH,
ABOVE THE RIVER DRAA

Hush, and be here, and
hold me like a cobra.
I'd gladly lie this way a few more
centuries, my fingers
knotted in your mane,
your pelvis twitching still in aftercome.
For the stars nailed our bodies together
with silver pins:
think of the lucid blitz our bodies made!
The sweat on your breastbone breathes like pine-resin,
the smell from your lap is white flowers.
And this will be the way we lie forever –
two lazy gods, gone rampant, here
at the top of the world.

Beneath us, the desert says nothing.
No presence stirs. The shadows come green.
But arching above the night, the sand, the burnished craters,
your panting traces birdwings in the sky.

DEATH OF A CHLEUCH DANCER

I burst into the marketplace
in time to see his face. It was sulphur-yellow.
They were lifting him from the ground, for he was dead;
the lover he betrayed
had murdered him. Now two men were holding the killer,
three kicked him, and one came behind with the dagger.
The crowd began to follow.

And I was left alone beside the blood, which
did not penetrate the dust, but lay and rippled.
And I called back many gentle words the dancer had spoken.
I remembered the smell of his body, wild honey it was.
And I thought of his bright blue hair, a banner and
pillow at night.
How should I
honour his memory?
I sat in the dust, destroyed, beside his blood,
and beat the flies away.

PITILESS AND ALONE

"This way for Darwin's tree ...
Straight on ... You're nearly there."
The Polynesians wouldn't stop their spiel.
But I was stunned by the peacock-blue of the ocean,
lapping its wide incessant tail in the sun.
I was dazzled and pissed off, I
couldn't be bothered listening. Even the giddily
fornicating doves were so much
buzzing in my ears.
It nettled me:
it wasn't for years of marriage, nor even good sex,
but just for a two-hour stand,
wham bam and thank you, a
dry rehearsal of lust,
that I'd been summoned here
by the fierce sexual presence of this
carnal, man-crazing, and wholly voluptuous landscape.

"That's her! The rubber tree. No no – over

here, sir. Five hundred years old,
and not a branch is withered!
How about that, sir – the same one Charlie Darwin saw,
and Fernand Magellan!..."
Well, here it was indeed, great surplus prop
from the final act of creation.
The sunlight skittered greenly off
ten thousand pocket-mirrors on its branches.
It *was* a rubber tree, and it was enormous,
big brother to the prophets and volcanoes.

But I kept looking back at paradise landscape:
the gardens in furious bloom below,
the lilting slopes, and the
flowering bay where stains of colour
spread on the water's face,
like blue and yellow irises I'd crushed between my fingers.
"Well?" I sniffed at one of my guides
and pointed at the tree,
"Doesn't the thing have flowers?"
"Of course it does," he said.
And from a spear-shaped sprout of leaves
he pried a swollen, reddish berry,
an oddly bifurcated thing,
and held it in the air like the jewels of a castrated animal.
"You think this is the fruit of the rubber tree – correct?
But you're wrong, you're wrong, it's the flower!
You hold it, please."
But I was already looking at something else.
"That doesn't interest me."
"Oh no?" His voice was sharper, and he pulled the berry apart.
"It has two sections, see?
The pistil's in one of them, here, and
the other holds the stamen and corolla.

Between them – a hard dividing wall."
He shoved it at me proudly.
"I see," I answered, taken aback,
"But how does the pollen get through the wall?"
"That's what they all want to know.
In the dividing wall there are
tunnels – holes the size of pinpricks, see?
And inside lives an invisible parasite,
smaller than a pinhead.
He feeds on the pollen
and carries it back and forth, stuck to his body –
the way a miller eats his bread
with flour stuck to his coat ... Now do you understand?"
He gave a smile of triumph, flicking
the berry to the ground,
and left me alone with the tree.

Humbly, with concentration,
I bent and raised the flower of the rubber tree,
and holding the carmine shell between my fingertips
I asked myself what Darwin would have made of it.
Where did it fit in the origin of species?
In the teeming uterus of creation,
how did parasite and flower find each other?
And before they did,
through all those millions of years,
how did one survive without the other?
Why didn't the parasite starve, become extinct?
Why didn't the flower die out, remaining barren?
And those pinpricks in the wall –
how did they get there?
Did a larger insect bore them, with a miniature brace and bit?
Or did the parasite just
happen along and find a handy wall, complete with holes?

Or else at dusk, on the fifth day of creation,
did a whole great platoon of marching parasites
halt before each rubber tree
in double column, the sergeant barking commands
as each invisible mite advanced to its post inside a flower?

I sat and mused like that, convinced
there is no system, no law; director and play
are equally witless and daft.
But then, quite idly, I raised the berry to my eyes, and all at once
a bolt of joy sluiced through me.
For I could see through the tiny holes, as if
through velvet-lined binoculars,
and dozens of colours were jostling and jigging in sunlight,
and everything was rockets and fireworks.
And I thought,
At last I've got him! –
the Lord of stones and berry-pips and men,
who sculpts the stars and vermin,
pitiless and alone,
who recedes from our vision faster than we strengthen our telescopes,
and surfaces in the fretwork of our veins.

That's him –
the One I never found, although I sought him
in Budapest, Vienna, New York.
It's him, old impresario of skies,
who planned this rendezvous for a quickie strip-down
so that once, and maybe once only, I might
behold in awe his naked presence,
director of all the fireworks –
so that this once I might vouchsafe applause
at the very quick of my being

to him who gave all things their birth and order,
and who, in the fullness of time, will detonate
all rockets, systems, and rubber trees, all stars
and me.

LOVE POEM TO HER, DYING

You've dozed off.
In the moonlight from the window
your chin is all bones and angles, like a corpse's.
I take your wrist again, and
try hypnosis.
"Don't die! Keep living. Want it because I want it!"
I've whispered the words a thousand times by now;
I whisper them again.
And as I repeat the spell
my eyes slide over your wasted frame once more, with the cruel
superiority of the living over the dead.

You used to think the soul
was an overnight guest in the body;
one day it would simply
step free, making its way in the new dimension.

But I was afraid that body and soul die together,
step by step,
the way you're dying now.
And nothing helps: not
x-rays, spells, not love or
medication – till
here you lie, adrift on a flimsy bed,

a small boat going under.
I hold a tattered rope, pathetic arm.
It slides from my hand.

WHITE MICE

"But they won't stop breeding, poor dears.
You'll have to do something, dear."
That was my wife. I had my orders. I marched:
across the kitchen, a pokey gait
like an executioner trying to get there late,
or a man who feels the crunch,
knowing the dust in his body is also not worth very much.

Good grief! the mice were
greeting me with
handstands, swan-dives, ski-jumps of joy.
Then, sniffing each other's bums,
they whizzed down their little slides, they caromed like
ping-pong balls with paws, tripping and
flipping and nipping themselves. And over here –
the raunchy little buggers! –
a gang-bang with fur.
It was worse than ancient Rome, it was like Sodom or Nineveh.

I grabbed the giant cage, and marched.
At the toilet, I turned it upside-down and shook,
and quickly pulled the chain, counting on
circular cleansing action.
No dice.
Those hundred mice held on to life
more firmly than the water held to them.

The whirlpool sucked and foamed; they kept
flashing by like horses leaping hurdles,
round and around like a pack of maniacal greyhounds,
and they jumped and spun in the spray like flying fish.
And me? I pulled the chain
again and again, I shook it, I
yanked the wretched thing but the flow had ended:
not one more drop descended.
And I stared at the dreadful splashing inside the bowl,
transfixed, until that lunatic
commotion in the swimming pool was still.
And then I stood some more and watched the feet,
the pink unmoving feet
that stretched out two by two beneath the glassy surface.

I was ready to bolt
when I noticed, on the toilet seat,
a sopping blob of fur –
a measly little mouse
that crouched and stared with small, red, grateful eyes,
and shivered like a sailor after a wreck.
I could have sworn, in all its drippy gratitude,
it was praying – praying to me, the master of mice,
who gave it this day its daily bread,
who fashioned for rodents
strong wheels for their delight, and spacious cages,
and whom, though he chose to flush them down the toilet,
it bore no grudge.

With its pink bird's-feet
it clung convulsively to the
toilet seat, staring up at my face
with a look of utter love.
I turned towards the wall

and shut both eyes,
till slowly I grew convinced
I was making the whole thing up:
there was no mouse there.

And then the feeling came: I was growing enormous,
like a man who carries the power of
God, and finds within himself
the dignity and cruelty it demands.
I drew myself up.
                  And yet I
shrank inside, I
shrivelled as I grew: couldn't I manage
one crummy little murder without becoming the victim?
For I'd seen, before my tight-shut eyes,
how each of those spinning mice was me.

My knees gave way; I gagged; I fled, straight
through the kitchen. Out in the yard
I held on to an apple tree
while still before me turned and whirled
the mouse's eyes, the mice's eyes,
and my vomit arced and splattered on my shirt,
and dribbled down the pants of the God of mice.

LORENZO DE' MEDICI

Careggi, with pomp: the zoo of the Medici.
Beside the tigers' cave, by imperial
whim and *fiat* of His Excellency,
a circular pond was built –
immense in size, as His Excellency commanded.

And in those days it was not yet understood
which species could coexist, and so they installed
God's plenty – releasing at random whatever
fishes and mammals and mixed amphibious creatures
could be had from merchant vessels emblazoned with
Venice ... Arabia ... Portugal ... tawny Levant ...

One day, towards dawn
(he rose before the birds),
the Medici entered the stillness of the Gardens
and paused by the pool. The water was black,
transparent. And on it a scarlet column:
himself, in scarlet.

A speckled fish was idling,
dropping her spawn by the shore. Behind her:
a predator – blue, pencil-thin.
She spawned ... He lunged ... And one by one by one
the young kept tumbling out to the waiting jaws.
Meanwhile, a moustachioed catfish
– shifty and vicious, a dead ringer for Frederick III –
was sipping yellow worms
like buttered macaroni from the slime.
Three yards away, the silver
kitchen-knives: zigzags in the murk.
And now a goldfish, already minus its tail,
came writhing in pain, arched like a
sickle between the tentacles of a polyp.
Nearing the shore it swayed
in the trough of two waves: striking, the way
the threads of white intestine wavered and played. And there
on the bottom, a lazy snail
stepped out for its morning constitutional.

Just then, from
the neighbouring villa, appeared
Marsilio Ficino, master scholar.
All night he'd fiddled and stitched, to get
one sentence from Plato right. And he: "Good
heavens, Lorenzo! You're pale as a ghost! What happened?"...
The eyes of the Prince were cold. He spoke
like a man coming back from another world. He said,
"I was imagining, Ficino, that I was God."

CHIEF CENSOR AND SECRETARY OF STATE FOR CULTURE HAN JU VISITS LI HO TO COMMISSION A POEM

The saucy stallions paw the air
With pomp and pearls and pommel-flare,
And beam the message everywhere:
    Let Li Ho make a poem!

The rings are gold, the banners blue,
The pennons dance like view halloo
As on they come in retinue:
    Let Li Ho make a poem!

The gowns that graze the reins above
Are lovelier than mourning doves.
The Censor brings a Censor's love
    And news of my commission!

And now the train is at the door.
And now they knock, and knock once more,

And chargers rear and servants roar:
     Their eyes are all on me!

I watch his halo, how it glows.
I wait to catch his first bons mots.
He even writes in rhyming prose,
     This genius from Chiang!

And neighbours say, behind their hands,
That God the Father botched His plans –
But Secretary-Censor Han
     Knew how to make corrections!

And now – he speaks to me out loud!
Why would a young man not be proud
And tumble down, completely cowed,
     When such a one takes notice?

My legs are water under me.
My mind is a catastrophe.
I'm shaky in the third degree
     And helpless in his sight!

And yet I know a thing to do.
This commissar was no one too
Until he learned whose bone to chew –
     As I can learn by heart!

The theme will touch on things of state:
"Though snakes are small, and dragons great,
Correct Ideas compensate."
One day I'll eat from this man's plate.
     Li Ho will make the poem!

from
SoCool

THE MYSTERY

Can't talk about it,
don't know if anybody else even gets it,
animals live in it, maybe they don't know it's there,
little kids the same;
grownups act oblivious – situation normal.
Half the time I just mooch along, then I laugh too loud.
But it catches me late at night, or in winter when
branches glow with snow against the bark, or some dumb old
song cracks me up and I want to go
howl in the city, or smash windows, or make my
life sheer shine in this miracle ache of a world.

THE MUSEUM OF DIRTY MINDS

The stuff that goes on in my mind, I wouldn't
feed it to a pit bull.
Fry it up, you could use it for toxic waste.
There's stuff I can't even tell you –
garbage thoughts, incredible video scenes;
how does it get in there?

But there must be a museum someplace for dirty minds:
WORLD'S ALL-TIME
FREAKS AND PERVS AND MENTAL MISBEGOTTENS.
I could give it to them.
I'd leave this carton at the door, with breathing holes
and a typed-up note: "Please find enclosed
one dirty mind. Take good care of it – din-dins at five; don't forget
walkies – and oh, by the way, kindly
strangle the filthy thing before it pollutes your Museum."

That'd show my mind.
Then I'd take off down the lane – no
mind/no problem.

POPPING PIMPLES IN THE PARK

We're popping pimples in the park,
Popping pimples after dark.

We pop them hot, we pop them cold,
We pop them when they're nine days old.

We pop them pink, we pop them yellow,
We pop them when they're fine and mellow.

We're soft-and-squeezy, over-easy,
Pimple-poppin' dandies!

CURSE AND FAREWELL

I won't go quiet at the bell
I won't go easy into hell
I'm not your pooch to buy and sell
I don't believe the lies you tell

I got an itchy little fuse
I got a gale force in my shoes
I got a supersonic force
I got a strike and no remorse

You're not the captain of my dream
You're not the coffee in my cream
So when your crummy life is through
Don't come to me to comfort you

I got a strike and no remorse
I got a supersonic force
I won't go quiet at the bell
I won't go easy into hell

DORKS FROM OUTER SPACE

Dorks are coming,
Dorks are near,
Dorks invade
The atmosphere.

Dizzy dorks
In party hats,
Dumbo dorks
With baseball bats,

In-line dorks
Who ram and slam,
On-line dorks
Like human spam,

Yakking dorks and
Dorkettes too,
Like a gabfest
At the zoo –

Dorks who garble
Every story,
Dorks galore and
Dorks in glory.

Dorks have landed,
Dorks are here,
Dorks infest
The atmosphere.

ME AND THE ULTIMATE SENSUAL EXPERIENCE

What can I tell you? Paradise gets leaky;
me too, and then you
wake up totally goobered. Stuck to your pj's.
Thing is, this is supposed to be the #1 thrill of your life,
and every time, I sleep through it.
If they had a contest on TV – "Tell Us Your
Ultimate Sensual Experience" –
I'd finish last.
"Uhh ... don't ask me, I was out like a light."

My ultimate sensual experience. Man, it's weird.
Maybe it's better with somebody else. But for now
it's this mystery place I go to, and then nothing but
leftover ecstasy stains. Some
absentee whiff.

Still, it's kind of cool, I guess – being a man and all.

THE SHAME

Among the thousand, or maybe the million things I know,
my all-time least favourite is this:
how shitty it feels, when you admire somebody
for their talent, or guts, or maybe just their
thoughtful way of getting through the day; anyway, as
I keep trying not to tell you, how shitty it feels when you
admire this person, and then some mean-
minded jerkoff starts badmouthing them behind their back,
and instead of sticking up for them – and
remember, this person has never done anything to hurt you –
you just stand there, while the cracks and cheap laughs get
meaner and hey you laugh too and
then, god help me I did I
joined in the trash brigade, I got off this
killer put-down, we all cracked up we were howling wc were
helpless with laughter and I walked away down the hall I was
caving in, I hated them all and myself I wanted to
break something, I walked and walked I felt so
helpless with shame, with the
shame.

RAINY DAY NIGHT

Creeks all run to the river
river runs to the sea
but nobody runs
nobody runs
nobody runs to me.

Hush you little darling
hush your sad refrain
the sky must weep, and you must sleep
and ache away the pain.

BACK WHEN I NEVER KNEW

Sometimes when the ache gets
too much, or my
friends start freaking and I'm not so cool myself,
or the whole world feels like it's sliding straight to ratshit –
sometimes I think back to a
bedtime long ago, I might have been four and my
mom still read to us; anyway, this one night
I stopped her, and I said the book out loud,
word for word, page-turn for page-turn, and it was
zap, it was perfect, it was all
pretend because the thing is, I still couldn't read.
But I was racing to big-kid freedom, just
chasing my runaway heart; I was chugging to
light in the grown-up world – coronas of
freefall light in the jumble and stations of growing. And I knew,
wherever I went, my mom would always be there …

Oh man, sometimes when the ache gets too much I
think back to then, back when I was so
hot to be older, and everything big was golden,
and the brand new world was waiting to show me secrets –
back when I never knew; I just
never knew.

ENOUGH

A tongueful of
    Music,
A lungful of
    Air,
A handful of
    Friends
With a heartful to
    Spare –

If ever I lose
    The knack of wonder,
Just shovel a grave
    And dig me under.

CHILDREN OF TOMORROW

When first they came around me,
    I was baffled what to do.
Their outlines were in shadow,
    And the sounds were shadowed too.

But soon the figures clarified,
    And murmurs turned to words,
And as they spoke, my heart half broke
    For this is what I heard:

We are the children of tomorrow.
We are the ones who come behind.
Earth is the dwelling place you borrow;
What home will we find?
What home will we find?

DEEPER

Often at night, sometimes
out in the snow or going into the music, the voice says,
"Deeper."
I don't know what it means.
Just, "Push it. Go further. Go deeper."
And when they come talking at me I get
antsy at times, but always the voice keeps saying,
"That is not it. Go deeper."
There is danger in this, also
breakaway hunches and I believe it can issue in
flickers of homing; but I
cannot command it, all I know is the one thing –
"Deeper. You must go further. You must go deeper."

JUNIPER AND BONE

Old momma teach me moonlight
Old momma teach me skin
Old momma teach me rhythm
When the ocean crashes in

And take me to the heartland
And teach me how to fear
Old momma teach me hunger
At the turning of the year

Old momma teach me music
Made of juniper and bone
Old momma teach me silence
In the certainty of stone.

Riffs

1

When I lurched like a rumour of want through the networks of plenty,
a me-shaped pang on the lam,
when I ghosted through lives like a headline, a scrap in the updraft,
and my mid-life wreckage was close & for keeps –

    when I watched the
    birches misting, pale spring
    voltage and
    not mine, nor mine, nor mine –

then: a
lady laid her touch among
me, gentle thing, for which I stand still
startled, gentle thing and feel the
ache begin again,
the onus of joy.

2

Nudge of her snuggled head
    against my shoulder,
cool of her flank
    beneath my finger-trails;
all night, all that
    prodigal night at the
tasks of
    passion –
sleep was the place we went,
    as the sun came through.

3

How
hooked I –
   honey how

   hooked &
horny; hooked and happy-go-honking
     – hey, how

   hooked on your
honey-sweet honey I
   am.

4

clean sheets

hot coffee in mugs

the woman I'm wild for:

   alive in the physical
   world – how come I

   been away so long ?

5

Yup, this is how it happens:
you do your half-smile, serious and bantering both,
and right on cue my insides
cave in, they go immaculately wingy ...

Now it's all coming back.
We're apart six hours and there's this
gravitational yank across the city: I would
drive through walls to get near you,
just to be near you ...

And also the way my body-glow
matches your body-
glow. Or how you flicker with
panic at being held – and I get the empathy bends,
exactly like I'm supposed to ...

Been a long time.

          I'd forgotten.

Gimme more.

6

Home-spooked
hotline.   Nobody's li'l number

one.   Big-eyed
radium child on stretched-out scrims of alert –

you could go off in my
life?... Well of

all

things!

7

I see you once, and it
happens all over again;
slip me a
hit of that wonky grin and there's rumours of
other – adulterous jostle of
unlived lives, hot possible me's on the prowl.

And when we sit down to gab, I get
babel and urspeak.
Sling us some
blues & true con-
cussions, pure jive on a wire: we're pulling
seismic flips and goofball acrobatics – and we
knew it all along!

Aw but when we lie down, it gets
utter. I tumble
head over hormone blur in a
crinkle of selves, sheer
sprong of expanded us:
ow-ooo!
We love like a backyard concert of perfect strays.

That's why I wrote you this note.
Wanna hold *your* up-from-lagoons, your
beamed-in-from-Mars bits, too.
Wanna let your many be.
                    (... And how will we
play it? like Bird? like no-trumps? darling, like movies of
speeded-up weather?

8

Ho hum you
said – so soon attuned
to ecstasy. Ho
hum, as if to say,
"Two weeks ago we barely
knew the peaks existed, now they're
rear-view postcard vistas."
Ho bloody hum! – till I cracked the
hubris/satori code: "Already it's
too good to last   /better
tempt fate fast   /take it for granted and past zip past zip past."

9

For months before we lay down
it kept going off, it kept going on
like blips & glory traces. Sub-
versive inklings of a way: the
way your tact and gags and libidinal gravity
seemed seamless in your body.
I loved the sense of yes you moved around in.

To me it meant (like a dare, and I got scared),
"The world didn't have to lose its tang?...
That deep, departed hunch of a life abounding –
that's still for real?...
There's plain brown joy on the hoof?"

(And then we laid-me-down. And got to know it.)

10

They
mock at me, poor
    sensibles –

"This time it's
    gonna hurt!"
But I can't

    change their pygmy
minds; sweet splash of
        dynamite, just

    graze on
me & you, the way we do, in
    late-20th-

century eden entry high.
                 (... Rare old
rendezvous on earth.

      Why else are we here?)

11

When you present
     your body and being and
utterly, bright-eyed
       companion –

and when we go deep into
     one another's eyes, and the
swim of communion is
ancient,
      ancient and grave –

or when you speak, not just of
     love but of
impediments to loving, and even that

serious caution inflames me: delicate
        scrunch of your shoulders,
    probe of your moral concern –

     how can such gifts undo me?
        Why does my system declare,
    Ha!
They'll never get out of paradise alive?

12

But she's gone – she's an
    ocean away, and

what is she
    dreaming?

13

Sweet christ, you are
lovely – over & over:

tonight I can nearly
taste it.   Track of your hopscotch your

quicksilver
trace in my

mind; wry bracketed giggle,
that triggers an ache at the

core; and over & over, new
sister & stranger your born-again

flow on my
tongue ...

Why aren't you here?

14

So I'll cook some
thump & witness, raise a
bumper car in the dictionary:

make up a real-
life us,
at play in the garden of words –

remember?

Not that we were good enough.
But there was this new and, yes foreknown astonishment:
somehow we were being actively permitted to live in our skins.

15

Those perfect
conversations, with their lazy
clarity uncoiling ...

Skin still homing to
skin, confederate across a
roomful of chatter ...

And fit of a life to a
lifetime: sedulous, incredulous, and OK downright
smug as we
basked around the block, two nerds in a blurt of summer ...

Doesn't anybody
know? we asked – not about us, about
acres of luminous storefronts, *camouflaged as storefronts*,
the sky in drag as sky, as blue as itself,
                                         and,
free for the taking,
all dirt & secrets of newly indigenous earth.
Plus our non-stop, gut-bucket grins.

Heaven *con carne*.

16

Hot po-
tato momma, got you in my

mouth all night.
Absenty

lady –
land o'

livin, I could pay my
rent all year & still owe dues.

17

Some kinda
stunts & wonders? Hocus-
focus? Hot cross

nerve ends?
Come on c'mon nice
lady, we ain't got all

lifetime!... Indefatigably adored one:

please to
appear on the sheet right now, called up by
succulent, shrink-wrapped, wholly refundable me.

18

Eerie
articulations of

love-
space:

delicate
angles:

arousal.

Will I
    trace this

deft a
    space upon your
body?

Would you be
                    here?

19

Wal, acey deucey
    trey divide –
I'm a guy
    with a fine wide-eyed

lady freckles too &
    squirms when she
feels good, I feel so
    good just

doin aw
    shucks
tricks an she's
    SOFISTIKATED!

20

Hey honey,
    it
sizzles.

Come closer, wanna
    see your
eyeballs roll!

Wanna
    tell ya
things ...

Don't like it, just
    don't come
in here – y'

    hear?

21

Capo and
fret, the
comical flesh
arrangements – flexed by
what rare
air, what gifted melody trace?

22

One thing
weird is,
    blowing

highwire struts of be-
    bop-a-
longing for

    lady in her moves, don't talk this
way – patrician
    dancer, no-

body's
    trick;
and has calm, and yes an olden chastity and whose

    pleasure is
classic, and breathes.

23

Six weeks of
plonk & longing?

riffs of
rendezvous with you?

I'm here to coin new nerve ends, fashion an
icon habitation, name of

be-when-my-reason-for-
being-is-snatched-away ...

    while you
    think some things through.

24

Oh babe!
when you come home, there'll be
mountains of hot patootie:
bow-ties and ice-cream,
could be a big parade.
And speeches – aw honey the
speeches will curl your ego;
talkin bout
lady of riffs &
backrubs, my lady of nowhere – said, the
damsel of cro-mignonne and the
life we're gonna lead
(big changes, chérie: *beeg* decisions) –

when you come home.

25

"Hello ... hullo? Yes it's
me – no no, there's no

problem, I just want to
change your life. So

look if you're
free tonight, could you

live with me?"

    (Come quick and we'll install

wet dreams in arcady, little donner &
vixen we'll rearrange the

continental mindset as
fallout & dandruff, and

oh,
by the way

could you
please be my baby – my

baby, my baby –
tonight?

26

I said I was
"happy"?... OK: so I
lied.

The forcible re-
construction of a
life,

caused by (woman, *deli-*
cado) the grave
assertion of your

pride, your need, your cells, your self-
donations in the dark – that is
not, re-

peat *not*
summed up by
"happy."

Try,
terror. Try, what I was born for. Try, whiff of
zero at the

core, in this claiming
sluice of utter
joy ...

Try,
how are we meant to live?

27

But if I
got un-

lucky once – meaning, if jiggers of neuron
delight flashed non-stop thru my

system yet I
had no hope of you, your

lissome stretch in bed, your
wit your gab your *areté* your life-on-the-line

embrace, sweet lean to graciousness your
curve in the mind your melt your fathoming goodness, gift of

wayward grace in a
giggle – if, I say if I

got unlucky for an hour and
lost you for a lifetime, one long

scan of dead
tomorrows if I

had no
hope of you ...

28

Hey funny thing, I had this
dream I dreamt you
came back here,

alive in my arms – not even your spiffy
clothes – but then I
woke and the sheet was drenched, it had loved-in

holes in it ...

29

Will pass your place.
Will think of us in
two-tone pandemonium,
performing the belly the breast,
performing the stations,

referring all calls to the wizard of waste not
want.   Your waist: your sultry waist.
My stupid want.

30

Multifarious dodos:
notably extinct –

gangs of ex-
es copped their snuff & split –

nobody wants to be nobody –

I just say I know you are fallible & gun-shy and still we could

occupy one planet

and look in tomorrow's mirror and start to brush *one two one two*

31

The angels'
cure for when they miss someone *very* bad is
    malt whiskey.

    'Dja
know that?
    I never knew that.

    Found out
my own way, special,
    just since you

    went away and to-
night at 2:48 A.M. I am
    practising up being an angel twinkle twinkle mud

32

Awright,
    jubilee:
le's pull off the
    mirror.

    You're looking like late-night
heaven.
    You're looking like rain.
You lookin like four on the floor & I thought I was hitching.

I thought we were quicksilver, now you're a
    ten-minute
coffee stop.

33

Hey, should I
talk
    sociology?

when where what how who?

All I
    want, woman, is
crawl up your left nostril & snuff it for keeps in sexual asthma heaven.

34

Music of
    methodist forebears.

Flesh inheritance.

I say these dreadful things for
    what I got left, I got rites of
ache & legacy.

35

So I'm too
    "obsessive,"
        huh? Too "wired to your moods"?...

Tonight our
        spats come back.   (Oh yeah:
      Return of the Wandering Spats.)

And sure: you cute, me
        addictive – but honey, you
                ain't seen nothin yet!

I got heartaches in real-time. Got this
                separation from hell,
      guilt with my kids, I got

two friends dead in a year my
                gallant parents soon and the nights, these
      plummeting dipso nights plus the

planet's shot – you're all I got left to
             hang on to.   You bet I
      hang on hard.

36

And not just that.

Most days, I'm

not obsessed *enough.*   For the

world sustains – it must! – a pour of

joy.   Somewhere, sanely past

wishing, it

rides into phase with the

news of its own largesse.

And bids us partake, calling,

Hey, last

chance to

dance!

last shot at flesh and danger!

For years I felt that hunger.

Yet always what I

ran from was the hunch, my well-planned

life the barricade – until two years ago I busted up my

life, to instigate a

blitz of deeper presence.

Just touch it, before I'm gone.

Since then, I'm a

freelance lightning rod,

hot for *tremendum.*

Since then I tote the yen like a sanctified growth – but shit, how

rarely I sustain it ...

C'mon, *you* know this stuff,

you're holy locus.

Don't say I'm "too intense," you jerk: you triggered grace-with-cleavage.

37

Honey, it's
so-oo heroic:

"hot for
tremendum."

All that leaves out is,
the drone of the rest of my life.

All it leaves out is
the doldrums of making a buck,

daily ego de-
bris, those non-stop misfires – oh

babe! – with a bevy of
red-hot maidens, bad trance of this

killer civilization, yeah,
the blahs the yays the blues the yack-yack-yack;

all it leaves out is the stoopit miles of missing you –
the (hi, maw!) muddle of me.

38

When you're up to yr
homburg in
hopeless, & the

damsel is not here –

what merrie cheer? zip zip no goddam cheer:

just
DIT-DAT-DOTS of biological/
ontological urgency –

pages of empties,
late-night lady reprise.

39

Pen-
ultimate lady, alive – sweet

skin and sesame:
why do we ever rub con-

tours, if not to conjure
shapes of what we aren't and

crave to be?...
Touching you I am

meat & pronto, I lounge in the chutzpah of
flesh; then woozy with

laughter and midnight and
caring, pure

carnal
panache – you, you, you in your frabjous parade –

how should I
reach for more?

Yet always behind you (this is
why I shy away), barely be-

yond you
is

nothing at all ...
Lady,

do not be offended when I
go there.

40

All the left-out
corners,

faeces of living, the
lint:

show me a riff with straight-up ejection & I want

those in too,
and count on your body to help.

41

Inch by
inch by inkling: niche by hunch.

Rock at my temples; sheer drop; fingertip
grips & a piss-poor attendance record in the daily adhesive world.

42

My
comrade of the
    ineffable:

    let me take you
down to
    logos:

    pre-
logos,
    where

    stones stone,
light lights,
    hurt things & people hurt and go on hurting.

43

Can't hold them together: –

We two were given to emerge
to absolute here and now;
it was plain & quirky, as
rooted in daylight as grass,
bright with its own green sheen and
when we go, our going will not diminish it –

And back on the planet, what news?
A single scene:
that 8-month child in Chile, electricity
up her vagina; the sergeant is
flicking the button; he waits, flicking & flicking to
make the parents inform but they *cannot*, they
never heard those names;
as well he knows.
               And
again: that 8-month child in Chile, the –

Vertiginous thoughtface.
Almost the heart goes missing.
Yet if I
deny the slaughterhouse
world, or if I deny the luminous presence,
something goes numb at the core.

But open-to-both is
mayhem –
nothing beside that child's – yet
falling apart with static and
origin   /incommensurable jangling   /what is, and what is.

44

Barely, be
mouth.

Mouth to self-
loathing:

kicks in the
abattoir ...

Mouth to
jags of

awkward, un-
prompted joy ...

Be mouth, and after that and what about us I
do not know.

45

If not for you,
I would be homeless in my going through the world.
It does not
attach you, but I have no good
person to lie down in – saving
yourself,
and the persuasion to.
If you hold to our jointure, I will be
strengthened in the holding that I do.

46

Your voice on my machine – and
I'm totalled, I'm
totally totalled again.

"... So
it's me – Miz
Plonk & Longing: remember
the wet wet witch of the West?"

Oh
babe, do I ever!
My heart so full of you ...
But *click!*, and you stopped.

Doxymoronic
darling, li'l breaded klutzlet:
get back here yesterday!
Gonna amorize you over 25 years, got some
full frontal loving to spare;

long distance love to spare,
from an ache with ears.

47

Take me again –
suite of longing, suite of

lies and
take me again.

48

Sweetheart: you gave me the
gift of ccstatic be-

longing, which is a
real live

piece of
shit ...

There you go – haring through
Europe with that

haemorrhoidal
twit, while I sit here hot for heaven &

re-runs on
flat earth and fucking im-

peccably up at
what pas-

ses for a
life?...

Belle beautiful lady; cardiac
angel; my

cystine Madonna – thanks a hairy
cluster!

May you rot in Buffalo.

49

But was I in
love with you, or with the
    image of your

    layabout love-
play, by
    bed-

    lamps magni-
fied on the
    ceilings of Literature?

    (... Gawd I said, I don't want
Literature I just want
    you &

    changed the ribbon.

50

It is
    possible:

you could be words and tomorrow –
    colony

homage, *aere perennius* and you still yodelling back,
    "No, no, let them

eat *my* cake if they're empty," as your
    figurehead recedes into red-shift anthology legends.

51

Smelting head foundries of ozone gravity breakage I
ached in a space and heard Keep keep keep

coming like something in flames
coming like nothing

coming like words are what a man could burn and burn in, and for keeps.

52

We swam into
paradise easy ...

That was in the flesh ...

Now it's
clobber & slop and
drag the jubilee hunch through a
busted language, you not
here.

53

Why else do I squat like a rain-
bow bruise in the night, arch-
ing in absence to you?...

It is for
lust. And
not just you!
    The
world that lay in blitz and bits stood

singlified to our ken. And if I
let the damn thing go, that
itch of a glory norm –

how would I breathe, in non-ecstatic time?

54

Three weeks.
No call.   No news.

Whadja think – I'm blind or something?
You're choosing him:
junk male incarnate.

And wherever you are tonight –
half-sloshed, skirt hiked, on your
back in some famous alley –
you've made your choice.

You had a crack at
sheer valhalla overdrive.

Now go piss up a rope.

55

Okay, I knew it was wrong.
    Over and over I asked you,
"What about him?
        doesn't it bother you?"

    But *oh no* –
  it was
      two different things, you said, it was
god knows what you said, you had all the answers ...

        Moon come soon.
    Big old moon like a
        plate of dogsick, and honey I'm tired,
     tired – I am so utterly

  tired of this slimy ribbon of
       lies, wound round my
    head, my
     shame my

too-long life to come ...

    Let's kill this now.

56

All
fall, desiring
desire, I
magnified her name.
This one is for lies.

This one is for
old-time-cheating lies. For
$A=D=U=L=T=E=R=Y$ lies.   This goes out for
101 Lessons in How to Lie to Yourself – meaning, first, those
oinks of eternal troth.
For the lie of her-husband-doesn't-have-soul,-so-it's-okay.

And on and on, the lie of a
love supreme when we
made it in toto six times, the lie of a
love made true by danger, memory lie of her
exquisite alleycat grace the lie of these
all-night
riffs & jackoffs this goes out for
months of a life gone missing, for
scotch black russian cinzano this one is for
cowardice lies, for
touch me and save me and us –

57

Roadkill love.
Reality meathook ruptures.

You know I
put my life in your keeping.

Jugular mercy.
Flick of your barbwire caress.

Wrongly, I guess – but
you told me you'd hold me forever.

Venom & blues.

58

Fact: it was
　　　　　　wrong from the start.
　　Our treks through plenary
　　　　skin and vistas, the
　blastoff to lovers' clear –
　　　　　　those were
　　　snotty renditions of soulful.
　Furtive.　　Self-serving.　　A lie.

　　　But if I gain
　　　　beatitude galore, and lose the gift of
moral discernment,
　　　　how real are my rarefied highs?
　　　　　　　If I teem with ecstatic
　　fulfilment but, bye-bye centre:
　　　　what good is my life?

　　　Deep source, dire
　　　origin: my
　　　　swarm of thoughts is
　　busywork, and what is real
　　　　exerts its steady terror.
　　The words are so much yack.
　　　　　　　I happen in the spaces.
But when my life goes mute again, tonight,
　　　　I have no place to be,
　　　　　　　except your deep,
　　　except your stark,
　　　　except your stern.

59

Maybe *you-and-me* was a lie.
But that big old easy place, where the

preternatural authority
flared out and, wham, it was

simply *a*
man and a woman:

that was
deeper than you-and-me ...

And okay, it's us that got mugged.
And a

lark and
a wrench and a lifetime.

But also, that
space of epochal

being is
shaped like home (even if

what? and where did it go?
are past my ken).   And now, though I

may not stay
bonded to you, by

reason of unclean union, still I
will not stop homing to

home.

60

It was bad.   Bad! It got
       bad, and
honey I'm sorry: I
           lost the beat.
       That stuff was garbage.

    But listen, your letter just came – and
we're gonna make it! got
           too much to lose ...

    So let's go
   back to the good part again;
     nothing is pure.

Back to
     he plus she and
electric ever after – please, back to our

       tantric
   buzz, the eros/
      lobotomy smorgasbord.

61

There were
coals of noel, hot bother & jeez, don't wanna

grab you for numinous stand-ins but honest to
edges got charred, fucken

wings half came off –
thought I was crocked & goners.

... Think I'd let go of
you, and heaven, now?

62

    Clear tracings in
empty space:

       from silence,

       nothing to
words to back to back to silence ...

    I could go
drunk into

       jive-time, the
emptiness, these halo lady

       tracings.

63

Look maw – no mind, and
I can

stick to the stony face of
nothing,

nothing-&-
you, and inch a-

head for one
more chomp on the root of *is*.

64

Stir me again.

I cd be hoisted *how* high, I cd be
god in a handcart: B L E E P.

Even the speechlessest rockface deigns to utter its pendant climbers.

65

One week to go: come
soonest.
Have walked some
planks since you been gone and now
would love to walk straight up the plank to
you arriving.
"Take that," I'd say, and hand you what has
happened since you left but I would
take it back awhile, lie down and
breathing slow beside you hope to
ease your eyelid stress and coming home.

66

Burning thru
altitudes of lifetime:
atmosphere very thin, me
very too. Fuel for outward, low –
back, a farce.

Signal if you are receiving this, otherwise ciao.

67

There is a pure
        over
load, & it

        copes
w/
        modernity ...

I want that. I also want
        chaucer and
water.

68

Just now I thought to your
doorway, you opened we
stood stock still in mind.
You were going to say, You *did* come but we
headed through the hall and
stood in the eerie surround – it was
locked, recalcitrant wholeness,
so shattering I felt
relieved we could not speak; we were almost
unmade to be together; we did not know,
Should things start here, or end? were we even a
ping on the face of silence?

69

So now you want me dead.
                    I
get the message.

        For months you had me
     hung by the heels and
        dripping;

                now it's
haul out the
            guts, & flush.

        So darling – Happy
     Returns! must be some
anniversary or other in the

                ghoul crusade.
     Maybe the first time you
        skewered me with your laugh. Or that deadly initial

        I love you,
     at dusk, in High Park. Or the soon-to-be-never-
                forgotten climax when you

        dumped me, you
     dumped me, you
                came back today and you

dumped me, bitch and
congrats!
            (And

thanks for the killer putdowns.
                    You butted me out ...

            Now I get to lick the ashtray.)

                    70

All that stuff it was monkey-grip jive your mean mean mind
who saw your chance and slid in fast you came for manhood
took it shook it trashed my self-respect – but you know I
never did like your body,
never those porridge thighs the spider scrawl around your eyes
right right every midnight wail about your body shape was true
those moves you made in bed old *Joy of Sex* retreads, my friends all used to
        yuck it up when I described them
and there was never a "sacred place" it was fake I winced at the slobbery
        gash of your mouth when you came
who was my hardon for living you made me crazy but I never loved your
        breasts
never drank your freefall mind didn't give me a buzz that talkie jive you
        really done me,
screwyou screwyou never craved your roadblock thighs your rehash moves
        in bed never did care for your flirt your flounce your paeans your mean
        mean knockout mind

71

"*Please,*
don't forget me."

... Please don't *forget* you?

Oh right: you were just about to
slip my foolish mind.
Thanks for the memo.

    (But tell you what.
    Stir the knife around – to the
    left now, a little bit lower –

    and you'll get not just the heart but also the heights the pits the
        drizzling shits & fun fun fun on Yonge Street Saturday night.)

72

Revved with
contagion, mumbling my

other names and re-
peat: Don't *know* this guy, just some

oddball goof wandered in for the sandwiches,
    for the body braille,
    for the heap big miniaturized cosmos itsy largesse.

[Stop all wired systems STOP.
Abandon all forms of pig-out epiphany addiction.]

73

SKID skid, dopey li'l
juggernaut;
Molotov sidecar momma, wrench me a frog.

If you got happiness tablets throw some out the window way down
opposite side.

74

Hey I scraped the
guywire limit – been so
high so long I don't know low from Lassie.
Ecstatic on empty.

(& if you are leastwise interested, think to
salute as I shoot straight past you CLONK go push down brown-eyed
daisies

75

Goin t'
      psych-
o whiteout count-
   ry, gonna

meet my baby there –

    She make a space I
      be there: nerve-
end wipeout, wired for sound –

Cash on my head, came barrelling thru off-
side splendours; fetched up
quaint in a dollop of hell.

    Humans cannot live here.

76

the stupid artillery of stars

moon a cold car-crash

snow piled high on the lawn and
me here sweating

face down in it,
fondling her name, and

puking   puking

77

Gone, it is
gone.   And I
make myself a lie, carrying on about it.

Time was I felt
clear meltdown in the flesh.
Gone: it is gone.

I could not hold to it gently enough; my
finger-clench blackened; the bruise.

                              Well, now I still turn, turn,
turn myself on in the dark – but what is to be done with

this pittance, my leftover life?

78

From one half-wasted by
bourgeois heaven & hell, and some tonight
would crawl 5 miles to be (mildly) discomfited so,
so taut is their agony –

say it:
whom do I pray to?
what do I centrally serve?

The 42 years of a selfish, directionless life,
halfway to goners now,
with its jerkoff highs, no right to even blaspheme ...

Scour me. Scour me, deepness, before I die.

79

Blood on
      behemoth.

Tracts of sheer
      unness.

Abyss and
      interludes.

I did that thing, I just can't walk home straight.

80

Egg-
shell

a-
live-o.

Still, a
live &

living live-
o ... Just

to be.

Piecemeal-

ly. Pang in bare
potency.

81

Get up eat fruit brew coffee,
do work see friends lie down.

Squeegeed in moments.
I am being squeegeed in detox moments. And all the

highs I can no longer afford –
irony, booze, hot transcendental crushes –

still throb like absentee limbs.

Get up. Do work. Lie down.

82

Rockface
    hallelujah.

Thought-
    high
emergence of

    foothold:

faithful

      : phrase.

83

No, please, not again:

Your voice on my machine –

and I'm
back in the heartspace of
lonely ...

But the season is
over: season of
flawless idolatry wank.

84

Byword, &
byword.
In beach-flesh

depths are
beings, under stone.

Us too. I barely shifted the silt of a comma.

85

Am going soon, but meanwhile I can hear
what mortals care for,
instep and desire.
Tell me what you cherish, won't
just walk; give me lifetime,
not renege.
I have no other use. Living I flubbed.
But mouth to mouth I could sometimes ache into words.

86

Deciduate, on grounds.

Am *a capella* palp.

What oncely greens is a light in the always-to-&-fro.

87

In her ... And
then we were home.

Our
breath bunched, the shudder – us

twined – of
(and if the) desire and the

planet
go on, the maybe tomorrows and

missing her   bad, though our

names and are

(written

wind

88

The dolphins of need be-
lie their shining traces.
Arcs in the air.

They do not mean to last. One
upward furrow, bright & the long disappearance,

as though by silver fiat of the sea.

The Mouse
and the Maid

THE MOUSE AND THE MAID

Epithalamium, for Susan

I

A dashing mouse, with a cool townhouse,
Was Minimus J. Magoo.
He lived by himself on the pantry shelf
At number Twenty-Two.

His parents were nice, but boring as rice.
His friends were barely awake.
Yet Minimus felt, beneath his pelt,
The soul of a rebel and rake:

For striding the streets in the snow and sleet
He never wore galoshes;
His bachelor pad was funky and bad,
With Brio and warm brioches;

And just for kicks, when up to his tricks,
He straightened his little toupee,
And he jumped in his wheels, and he kicked up his heels
And he painted the suburbs grey.

II

His hero was Abe, with his sister Mabe,
And Abe was the Deli Prince,
And frequently Mini, when out on a whinny,
Would tool on down for a blintz.

And Abe and the boys would holler, "Ahoy!"
When Minimus J. rolled in,
For he was as strange, as dramatic a change
To them as they to him.

And lounging there in the musky air,
Swapping the news and sports,
He'd gaze at the knishes and bagels and kishkas,
The latkes and liver and borscht,

And he'd think, "Oh dear!" (with a muffled tear,
Which he never revealed to Abe) –
For bright as a coal, there burned in his soul
The love of a mouse for a Mabe.

III

Now, Mabe had eyes like blueberry pies
And hair like a waterfall,
And Minimus J. gave his heart away,
His paws and his whiskers and all.

Yet Minimus Mouse had sought for a spouse
Since he was barely two,
And no one he'd met, not a candidate yet,
Had cherished the real Magoo;

So why should a lass with comestible class,
Exotic, yet modest and trim,
With suitors galore at the window and door,
Consent to be wooed by him?

"What," he'd demand, "If she thinks I'm bland?
Or boring? or mousy? or square?"

And glumly he'd curse, crying, "Darn it!" and worse,
And slump in the musky air.

IV

The suitors! the suitors! They came like commuters
In buses and pickups and carts!
For Abe was the Prince of the Kensington Blintz,
But Mabe was the queen of hearts.

The word had gone out for miles about,
The nosh at the Deli was grand –
But grander yet, in the bachelor set,
Was the hope of the sister's hand,

So through the door they streamed galore
To preen and strut their paces,
Telling her jokes, and giving her pokes,
And filling up their faces.

But Mabe, with the mien of a gypsy queen,
Served each alike in the house –
Though once in the crowd, as Minimus bowed,
She murmured, "Who's the mouse?"

V

First once a week, then twice a week,
Then every second day,
Addressed to Abe, but meant for Mabe,
A parcel found its way:

A matchbox, squeezed with ham and cheese,
Would somehow appear at the Deli;

Or a pile of Ritz and bacon bits
In cellophane, scented with jelly;

Or a lipstick, a thimble, a Valentine symbol –
And each inscribed in a blue
And meticulous hand: *Your slave to command,
Sincerely, You-know-who.*

And grimacing, Abe, with a glance at Mabe,
Would stow it behind the grill.
And silently Mabe, without looking at Abe,
Would slice another dill.

VI

But the suitors! the suitors! They swarmed like freebooters,
They turned her life to hell;
For Abe, though a prince, was firmly convinced
That sisters should marry well.

And daily he pressed, "Pick out the best –
Like Harvey, or Meyer, or Fred."
And Mabe would protest, "If those are the best,
I'll marry myself instead.

"They come to swill at the grill and the till,
They're hot to snaffle a wife,
But where can a wench discover a mensch
To cherish the rest of her life?

"Find me a man, not a flash in the pan,
With a heart like a big roomy house.
As long as the heroes are machos or zeros,
I'd rather marry a mouse!"

VII

Now, today was the day that Minimus J.
Had chosen to settle his fate:
To invocate Abe, "Would you supplicate Mabe
To live as my married mate?"

But when he stepped into the restaurant's din –
The clock stood high at noon –
The very words that we recently heard
Were echoing round the room.

In the blink of an eye, the mouse chirped, "Hi!"
And tootled toward his choice –
To meet with the throb of an angry mob
And the roar of their single voice.

The suitors! the suitors! Like manic computers
They spat out their envy and hate –
Till a fateful cry rose clear and high,
And Mabe came wailing: "WAIT!"

VIII

Dear Reader,

It's time that the metre and rhyme give way to sober prose – or else the sense of mounting suspense may bring our cast to blows. (For metrical writing is known for inciting dramatis personae to crime, while bathos and loot are the frequent pursuit of characters crazed by rhyme.)

And yet, I confess, an additional stress persuades me to suspend it: as I contemplate the story to date, I don't know how to end it.

Does Minimus J. (as I hope) win the day? Will true love conquer all? Or is this a scene where the Guillotine of Fate must finally fall?

But with your aid, a choice can be made: in post-modernity, the reader's rights and the writer's rites can profitably agree.

Viz:

- If you'll kindly look at the back of the book, a ballot awaits in a slot.
- On the ballot, a blank: the author will thank the reader for ending the plot.
- To enter an Ending, just mail (without bending) your climax to this address, where plots will be counted by teams of accountants, and literacy assessed.
- The unspoiled plots will be sorted in lots, perused to the final line;
- And the Ending voiced as the popular choice will stand as Section —

IX (a)

The fateful cry rose clear and high,
And echoed throughout the land:
"A mouse may dream of a love supreme –
And a mouse shall have my hand!"

Across the floor, and out the door,
And high to the sky serene
In the whirlaway noon of their honeymoon
A trail of gold could be seen:

Through dawns of roving, through skies of love,
Through memory sunsets they sped,
And every night on a field of delight
They spread their darkling bed.

And the years went by in the distant sky
Till they shone with love as they played –
And star-gazers christened the new apparition:
Maximus Mouse and the Maid.

IX (b)

The fateful cry rose clear and high,
As Mabe blurted out with a wrench,
"He isn't a man – he may be a mouse –
But he, uh, seems to be a mensch;

"I'll have him, I guess." This qualified Yes
Brought Minimus J. to her side,
And they scuttled away on the very next day,
A blushing mouse and his bride.

But sad to report, their bliss was short,
For capitalism reigned;
Ten mouths to feed, a mortgage deed,
And love went down the drain.

The house repossessed, divorce came next,
And nights in a gambling casino,
Till the mouse took a stand for the working man
And Mabe flew off to Reno.

IX (c)

The fateful cry rose clear and high,
"Remove the rodent *now*!
If it ever sneaks back, I'll hack and I'll whack
Till it looks like a plate of chow!

"Who wants to marry a critter that's hairy,
And squirmy, and bland, and smelly?"
And the suitors took scissors and chopped off its whiskers
And frog-marched it out of the Deli ...

Through streets of sorrow, with no tomorrow,
Through nights where spectres thronged,
A broken mouse without a spouse
Went lonesome, lost, and wronged,

Haunting the spots where love is bought,
Its features sickly pale,
Till at the last, in a blizzard's blast
It passed beyond the veil.

X

Dear Reader, you'll see by our (a), (b), and (c),
The balloting led to a tie,
And I'm quite mortified, but I still can't decide
Which ending, if any, to try;

And meanwhile, back at the Deli, a pack
Of characters cool their heels,
Asking their friends how the story ends
And when to deliver their spiels.

But though the plot appears to be shot,
I'll tell you as much as I know:
"Meyer and Harvey went off to pick larvae
While Fred took up the banjo,

"And Abe, who was Prince of the Kensington Blintz
(Did I mention the fact above?),
Opened a franchise, profited branch-wise,
And married a waitress for love.

THE END."

CODA

The Deli at last has been cleared of the cast –
Only the lovers are there,
And the fateful trill of "WAIT!", which still
Resounds in the musky air.

And the moment dilates, and the big clock waits,
And Mabe gives a quizzical smile,
And Minimus stands with his life in his hands
And lets it breathe a while.

There's nothing to say, and they seem to sway
Within a perpetual now,
Where borscht and a bittersweet wisdom fit
In consonance somehow.

And who can trace the difficult grace
Of a story's end? Not me.
Yet still they stand, in the near-at-hand
Of the things that are yet to be.

Not Abstract
Harmonies But

400: COMING HOME

You are on the highway and the great light of
noon comes over the asphalt, the gravelled
shoulders. You are on the highway, there is a kind of
laughter, the cars pound
south. Over your shoulder the scrub-grass, the fences,
the fields wait patiently as though someone
believed in them. The light has laid it
upon them. One
crow scrawks. The edges
take care of themselves, there is
no strain, you can almost hear it, you
inhabit it.

Back in the city, many things you once lived for
are coming apart.
Transistor rock still fills
back yards, in the parks young men do things to
Hondas; there will be
heat lightning, beer on the porches, goings on.
That is not it.

And you are still on the highway. There are no
houses, no farms. Across the median, past the swish and thud of the
northbound cars, beyond the opposite fences,
the fields, the
climbing escarpment, solitary in the
bright eye of the sun the
birches dance, and they

dance. They have
their reasons. You do not know
anything.
Cicadas call now, in the darkening swollen air there is dust
in your nostrils; a
kind of laughter; you are still on the highway.

THE MORNING OF THE SECOND DAY

How will you handle my body?
What will I do to your name?
New selves kept tramping through me like a
herd of signatures, I mislaid
sentences halfway, the trademark was *ummm* ...?
Which one of me did you want?

Hey but that was another life, and donning the
one-way flesh, now glad and
half at home at last in the set of your neck,
the carriage of your thighs, I believe I sense
the difficult singularity of the man I
am not ready for.

But how will you handle my body?
Some day ten years from now we'll both
wake up, and stretch, and stare at somebody's ceiling –
our own, sweet jesus our *very own ceiling!* – and boggle, with
ten-year thoughts in mind.
Look out, I believe we're married & lap your
hair across my face, this must make sense but what will I
do to your beautiful name?

Night and day it
goes on, it goes
on. I hear what feel like ponderous immaculate
lizards moving through; I call it
absence I call it silence but often I am
glad for the wrong reasons.
Many times at 6:00 A.M. there is a
fiendish din of cans, like now
for instance and we
lunge up punctured through the
blur & the broken
glass of last night's argument, fetching up
groggy on a landscape of bed, well I can
taste our dubious breath and look it's
me, babe, I wabble my neck and lounge the
trophy from my dream across your belly, your
body slouches towards me, jesus, there is
something about our lives that
doesn't make sense, tomorrow
I'll fix them up, remind me, the garbage
cans have stopped now but the room is
bright too bright to
fix I mean ah jesus I burrow slow
motion back to sleep; and the
lizards resume their
phosphorescent progress, I crowd towards them but I should
not be here now, swallowing fast & doggedly gawking &
staying put and glad but glad for the wrong reasons.

HE ASKS HER

What kind of
    pickle were we in? Every
piddling triumph I dragged into the house –
                                   by the ears
    ("I fixed the washer in the outside tap.")
by the snout
    ("I sold another book today. That makes eleven.")
or by the curly Q of its little pink tale
    ("I seduced Madame Nhu this aft. In the john at Eglinton station.")
               – they all became weapons in the stockpile.
Sometimes I trickled under the door to tell you
    sometimes I walked thru the wall, all shucks & left-handed
sometimes I'd bound in via the second-storey window, hanging by my
    canine incisors.
But what kind of
    pickle were we in? You had to
turn and finger the miserable little feat,
    testing the cutting edge on your own flesh,
and I would savour the way something
               closed inside me and fondled itself,
knowing that soon you'd be
    cast down again, that I would be rejected.

RECOLLECTION

I remember still
    a gentle girl, just married, how she
drew her husband down, they had
    no practice but she gave him warm
openings till he became a

cocky simpleton inside her,
coming like kingdom come for the excellent
pleasure it made in their bodies.

WHEN IT IS OVER

The low-light recedes, the records recede, skin
    empties. Under my eyes
your eyes recede, I brush your cheek you feel what
    touch what clumsy much-loved man
receding? Your body is full of listening,
    exquisite among its own
shockwaves.   So. What
    space are you going into?

Over & over, love, what other
    music? Your
eyelids will be here for
    centuries, do not come to.
But flicker, come deeper, let be – the jubilation
    eases through your
body.   So. What
    space have you gone into?

Slowly, love, beneath me
    your breathing returns.
Now it is over, the flesh and resonance that filled that
    other space do not come to and
try to tell me where, for it is over.
    But drowse off now; as the after-pleasure settles
gently into our lives, it is over and
    over, and over, and over, and over and over.

That one is me too – belting thru
    school to the rhythms of glory, tripping,
        blinking at vanishing place-names
    Etobicoke   Muskoka   Labrador   then Notting Hill Gate but
        he could never keep them straight,
    though as they ran together they always had
        people in them, like ketchup on his shirt.
    Extra-gang spikers and singalong, I believe that was
        Labrador?   Teachers.   That
    girl in Stockholm – Christ! what did they
        expect? the man was otherwise engaged.

For there were treks, attacks and
        tribal migrations of meaning, wow
    careening thru his skull, the doves &
        dodos that descended, scary
    partnerships with God, new selves erupting
        messianic daily – all the grand
    adrenalin parade!
        He was supposed to wear matching socks?

It was a messy pubescent
        surfeit of selves but there were
    three I didn't know about,
        the sabotage kids.
    They never budged.
One was perpetually leaving his
        penis behind in garbage bags. One had a
    bazooka stuck in his throat, hence had some
        difficulty speaking.
    The third would sob all night in the lonesome night,
        crying for something damp, and close, and warm.

I came across them far too late.
They kept on dousing
epiphanies, misdirecting traffic.
They kept on daring me to
break down, like a carburetor with a passion for wildflowers.

HEAVEN AND EARTH

Ordinary   moving
stoplight & manhole
maple tree   birch tree   oak
dandelions   crabgrass
ferry boats   Andromeda
fathers   and mothers, and
heaven and earth and all
vivacious things that
throng around a man
will not approach until he
hears himself pronounce "I
hate you" with his body.

BRUNSWICK AVENUE

We are in
bed, the dark is close to my face. Hilary
moans in the crib. It is getting
warm in here, the covers are
close, I am going
into it.

All the long-legged suns have clotted again
in my head, and only keyholes know a song.
Emptiness is my alibi, but it is pitted with syllables like
caterpillars moving hoarsely across the face of the Bible.

Outside, the rasp of a snow-shovel
grates in the dark.
Lovely
sound, I hang onto it. In the
stillness I feel the flakes and the heft of
that man's left arm, and the sudden
twinge as the shovel lets go of the wet snow I am going into it.

Many spaces no longer belong to the ones who once filled them.
The air keeps striding through.
Pinholes arrive & open like sprayguns, and always
the long-legged suns are combining.

Beside me on the bed the woman with whom I did
great violence for years, preserving
dalliance and stigmata, stretches
easy in her after-pleasure, sleeping.
Clothes and our wetness load the air.
Her hair is on my shoulder.
The covers lift and fold, and the shovel scrapes and I hear the
endless holes in the night hang down and the snow and our fragile breathing.

Whatever I say, woman,
it is not that
I say our lives are working – but feel the
ambush of soft air – nor that our
rancour & precious remorse can be
surrendered merely because the earth has taken
green dominion here, beneath us
the belly of grass is real; and lady,
it is not that
lovers by the score come sporting
fantasies like we had, strolling
bright-eyed past the portulaca – we could
whisper messages, they would be
snarls in our own blood;
and I am
bitter about our reconciliations, we panicked, we
snowed ourselves each time. So lady,
it is not that
I hanker for new beginnings – confession and
copout, we know that game; it's as real as the
whiskey, the fights, the pills.
And I do not start this now because the grass is green,
and not because in front of us the
path makes stately patterns down the slope to Grenadier,
and all the
random ambling of the couples hangs
like courtly bygones in the shining air;
the old longing is there, it always will but I will not
allow it.

But there is
you, lady. I

want you to
        be, and I want you.
            (Lie here on the grass beside me;
                hear me tie my tongue in knots.)
I can't talk brave palaver like
            I did ten years ago – I
        used up all the words – but now I
    sense my centre in these new
        gropings, wary, near yours, woman,
            coming to
                difficult sanities.

        I want to be here.

IN A BAD TIME

So much is gone now, bright and suicidal,
so much is on the verge.

What good are words among the
rock, the glittering wreckage?

Fallout falls; the empires breed
the nightmares that they need.

The only words are lives.
Friend.   Friend.

NIGHT

Night one more time, the darkness
close out there on the snow.
Goddamn war, goddamn smog, close the blind.

How many times have you
stared through that window at darkness?
Come on over here, lie on top of me, let's fuck.

Good men would think twice
about it, they would
not be born in this century.

Night one more time, great
lobotomy. Come on over here with your body, lie down, tomorrow
it all starts again.

COMING BACK

Saying crabgrass, plantain, begonia,
saying Queen Anne's lace, devil's paint-brush, flag.

Time I was young I thought
letting them go was holy.

Quartz, saying granite, saying dirt-farm, outcrop,
limestone, fossil, saying shale.

Coming back who needs it – giving up the
things I never owned?

Saying city, chevvy, collision the sirens;
hungry, saying finger, saying food.

WORDS FOR THE GIVEN

If I take up space in the silence, master, friend –
let it be, we all live here and do not matter.

So I did my shabby trick again; we
both saw it happen, I won't get away with it.

And nothing is enough.   I did not say that
for content, it was a greeting.

No listen, I still don't know but what does that
matter? Listen.   It is.   It is.   It is.

SIBELIUS PARK

I

Walking north from his other lives in a fine rain
            through the high-rise pavilion on Walmer
lost in the vague turbulence he harbours
            Rochdale   Anansi   how many
        routine wipeouts has he performed since he was born
                                    and mostly himself;
                drifting north to the three-storey
        turrets & gables, the squiggles and arches and
baleful asymmetric glare of the houses he loves

Toronto gothic
walking north in the fine rain, trudging home through the
      late afternoon,
    he comes to Sibelius Park.
Across that green expanse he sees
      the cars parked close, every second licence yankee, he thinks of
the war and the young men dodging, his wife inside
    with her counsel   her second thoughts
        and the children, needing more than they can give.
And behind him, five blocks south, his other lives
  in rainy limbo till tomorrow:
    Rochdale, yes   Anansi
      the fine iconic books, sheepish errata
        shitwork in a cold basement, moody
      triumphs of the mind
        hassling printers   hassling banks
    and the grim dudgeon with friends – men with
deep combative egos, driven men, they cannot sit still, they go on
      brooding on Mao   on Gandhi
and they cannot resolve their lives but together they make up
        emblems of a unified civilization,
    the fine iconic books;
          he is rooted in books and in
that other place, where icons come alive among the faulty
    heroes & copouts, groping for some new tension of
    mind and life, casting the type in their own
    warm flesh
        hassling builders   hassling banks
and he is constantly coming and
      going away, appalled by the power of
    wishful affirmations, he thinks of the war, he
hears himself 10 years ago affirming his faith in Christ
    in the lockers, still half-clasped in pads & a furtive
      virgin still, flailing the

lukewarm school with rumours of God,
              gunning for psychic opponents
though he could not hit his father and what
                        broke at last was the
     holiness; and he can't go back there any more
without hearing the livelong flourish
          of Christ in his mouth, always he tasted His funny
taste in every arraignment but it was himself he was burying.
And the same struggle goes on and when
                    he drinks too much, or cannot sleep for his body's
     jaundiced repose he can scarcely read a word he's written,
          though the words are just but his life has the
funny taste, and the work pulls back and
                              snickers when he begins.

And then Sibelius Park!
          The grass is wet, it
     gleams, across the park's wide
               vista the lanes of ornamental
     shrub come breathing and the sun has filled the
               rinsed air till the green goes luminous and it does it
                                   does, it comes clear!

                    I I

Supper is over, I sit
          holed up in my study. I have
no answers again, and I do not trust the
     simplicities, nor Sibelius Park;
                         I am not to be trusted with them.

But I rest in one thing. The play of
          dusk and atmospherics, the beautiful rites of
     synaesthesia, are not to be believed;

but that grisly counter-presence, the warfare in the lockers,
myself against myself, the years of desperate affirmation and
    the dank manholes of ego which stink when they
come free at last –
                    the seamy underside of every stiff
    iconic self – which are hard   which are welcome
are no more real than that unreal man who stood and took them in;
    are no more real than the glib epiphanies,
                    though they ache to bring them down.

For they are all given, they are not
    to be believed but constantly
they are being
    given, moment by moment, the icons and what they
suppress, here and
    here and though they are not real they have their own real
presence, like a mirror in the grass and in the
    bodies we live in we are
acceptable.

There is nothing to be afraid of.

PART II

NOT ABSTRACT HARMONIES BUT

I

Well: I used to be young and –
sensitive?! hoo boy, you know I
lay awake all night and dreamed of dying,
like any young man should. Felt
good. Kept the sheets dry.
But now I trim my beard in a rumour of white,
and my body starts grumbling earlier in the day,
and I would not be young again for a finished Ph.D.
For the young keep doing it; they don a fearful
abstraction, and deliver themselves from
appetites and earth
with geriatric haste.
But I, being lately recovered, choose never
in thought or word or deed
to totter back to the kingdom of the young.

My driven twenties – why are they such a
rueful nightmare now?
I guess because our lives were abstract.
My friends'. My own.
They left out
squawky imperfect flesh and the way things are on the planet.
And though we were first to discover
freedom, fellatio, zen, and the class analysis,
like bantam Einsteins solemnly arriving at the
wheel in '65 – which was

fair enough, how
          else is wisdom renewed? and often we made
   brave lives ourselves – yet all of it was abstract!
                For it served the one forbidden god,
                          denial of here and now;
and I honour high abstraction but never stop being
          various, earth and companions! and
                              gritty, and here and till we can
             cherish what surrounds us, loathe it and
                   cherish it we will only
          oppress it further with all our heady perfect systems.

                              I I

                   How did I
                      miss it? that
                   haltingly, silently,
                         stubbornly, home,
             each mortal being announces the pitch of itself
                   in a piecemeal world. And
             here! it was always here, the living coherence.
             Not abstract harmonies but, rather, that
   each thing gropes to be itself in time and what is lovely
is how, once brought to a pitch, it holds & presides
             in the fragile hum of its own galvanic being.
                   And more: as it persists it tunes to
          every thing that is, neither in outright
                      concord nor yammer but half alive on
             all those jumbled wave-lengths,
                         inciting a field of near-coherence
                   in the spacey surround.

                   One luminous deed, amid the daily
          gumbo of motives; a well-made

journey, or tree, or
law; a much-loved parent; the fullness of grief –
whatever: let that
flourish in its completeness,
and every nearby thing begins to
quicken, tingle, dispose itself in relation,
till smack in the clobber & flux,
coherence is born ...
So each live thing endures,
rife with the itch to pick up
currents that do not mesh and
live their concert – *each* thing, which makes for a
welter of harmonies, until those
jagged cadenzas of meaning
ripple like simultaneous fields of light.

And if a man could stay
clear enough, stay near and distanced enough,
resonance by resonance it would ease down into itself, coherences
cohering till almost he senses
the world as jubilee: I mean
the hymn of the fullness of being –
the ripple of luminous cosmoi, up/down &
across the scales of
orchestration in many-
dimensional play, here good now bad but
telling the grace of daily infinite coherence.

III

I speak of full coherence
in hope alone; I am not that
quickened attender, and have no mind to
loll in a blissed-out stupor,

while bodies are tortured or starve.
Yet though it is
never achieved in our lives it is
never wholly absent, for always we are
buzzing on the verge, excited by
urgent currents that fret us & rev us and
never quite jibe with our own and in a
piecemeal world, let this be what I
dwell in: not
abstract harmonies, but rather the
chronic, abrasive not-quite-
consonance of the
things which are.

And the jangle is hard, but not to be quickened is death.
And we are a botch and a warmup, although
I do not know for what,
and who tunes us – if it can be
said that way at all – is an endless vocation.

ON A KAZOO

Wal   I got a gal
on my   kazoo
and she looks real good
like a good gal
should,
singin
high
on a wire all
day.
Hey!

I got a fly
in my   little eye
        an it's buzzin right around
till I seen that
                        sound,
        singin
                high on a
                wire all
                                day.
                Hey!

        I
                got a
        lady
                an a
        lady got me;   an I'm
gonna play around
                        with her *sweet right*
                knee!
        Singin
                high on a wire all day.
                                        Hey!
                Stay
        high on a wire all day!

LAY DOWN

        I guess it's
half the way you lay down and you
                lay down easy, girl, it gives me
        room to be beside you.
                                Every

time inside your
                    body –
         hey,
     surprise again: we
            fit!

             The rest of our lives in
         bed with us and
                         doesn't it feel good?
              Crowded here but fine, the way we lay down.

             Wear you like a
         lifetime, girl, don't mind me –
                    just sweeping up the bed, I'm
         only the preacher, yup,
                            at

home again the way we lay down there's also your #&%*! jokes.

     YIP YIP

         I love the way

     your steady field can jostle
                    cells in who I am,
         over & over

     some odd familiar blueprint
                    shifts into place among me, till old
         molecules, old
                    hangups,
         old desires –

all lean one way, a new one, singing
        Yip yip kadoodle   */in the squiffy universe*

    and I don't quite get the words but I
        believe I'll stick around. And
I – but

    who is
        'I'?

    Aw
never mind, forget
    that part, just
keep
    being ...

(I love this woozy feeling when she stands there

OF EROS, IN SHINY DEGREE

Ah, how the body
Tracks its desire
Thru the bones of the living;
Jesus will tire,

America's empire
Will buckle and fold:
The will of the body
Does not grow old.

All that men longed for
Built and destroyed

Greece and Golgotha
Parmenides, Freud

Pithecanthropus
And serfs in their throng
Instinctual murder
Instinctual song

By brute generation
By sainthood, by strife
Alive in their bodies
They hungered for life.

A nation could choke
And choose death at the source –
Still rife in the planet
Desire would course.

The choice of my people
Occurs and is gone.
I lie in your body.
The current goes on.

WHEN FIRST I LAY

When first I lay   in your sweet
                body, woman   girl
I had no mind to settle down in someone's longing.
Not one more time   I was hair-trigger, girl, and do not
           gentle me too much, it feels like dying.

You laid my dust   and skittish

itch to go and hide;
I never knew how much I hurt until you eased me.
Come on come on –   you got me laughing in my sleep, I never
laughed that deep in years, I'm from Toronto.

You let me be   sometimes you
came apart, like me
and still the quiet, awesome mesh of us goes on.
It boggles me   it's not our doing, girl, and yet this
hale unlikely space connects around us.

When first I lay   in your sweet
lifetime, woman   girl
and counted bruises every time your loving touched me,
you let me be   half-spooked for sure and laughing, till the
words came real, that
being here is home.

REMEMBER, WOMAN

Remember, woman, how we lay
Beside ourselves the livelong day
And tuned out all that heady fuss
And felt new lives invading us?

We loved, as though our bodies meant
To fire their own enlightenment,
And raise, despite our moral dread,
A carnal OM on a rumpled bed.

Remember how the light that shone
Spilled from within you? Off and on

The switch was easy, and we lit
Eternal brightness for a bit;

And me, I was so tightly strung
I could have pulled myself and rung,
Or pealed out gratis from the glans
A paradise for puritans.

Brothers, lovers, mothers, wives –
Glad ambush by a dozen lives.
Fresh selves of you, new many me,
A sacrament of letting be.

And loved on, in a bell-jar hush –
Ankle, breast and burning bush
The flesh was common, and we strayed
Ecstatic in our own parade.

Cocky beatitude! which sank
To getting by in brain and flank.
The fire went out; our lives grew sane.
Sweet Christ, I long for then again.

YOU CAN CLIMB DOWN NOW

                    Forgive me that I
ask too much of your
                    body,
            boosting sweet day-to-day flesh into
                    Endless Redemption by Passion.
            Must be a

drag up there, and you can
climb down now.

If only something could
centre us.
One
whiff of carnal joy and a man will come unhinged,
or try to cram the body of his longing
thru somebody's flesh into heaven,
to never be lonesome again.

Aw, you must get
tired up there, those crummy wings & you
don't look good in marble.
You can climb
down now, girl, I
like you more in person – though I
willed you there. I
nailed you there.
Forgive me.

THE GODS

I

Who, now, can speak of gods –
their strokes and carnal voltage,
old ripples of presence   a space ago
archaic eddies of being?

Perhaps a saint could speak their names.
Or maybe some

noble claustrophobic spirit,
crazed by the flash and
vacuum of modernity,
could reach back, ripe for
gods and a hot lobotomy.
But being none of these, I sit
bemused by the sound of the word.
For a man no longer moves
through coiled ejaculations of meaning;
we live within
equations, models, paradigms
which deaden the world, and now in our
heads, though less in our inconsistent lives,
the tickle of cosmos is gone.
Though what would a god be like?
Would he know about D N A molecules? and
keep little haloes, for when they behaved?...
It is not from simple derision
that the imagination snickers;
but faced with an alien reality it
stammers, it races & churns for
want of a common syntax and,
lacking a possible language,
who now can speak of gods? for random example
a bear to our ancestors, and even to
grope in a pristine hunch back to that way of being on earth
is nearly beyond me.

I I

And yet
in the middle of one more day, in a clearing maybe   sheer
godforce
calm on the lope of its pads

furred   hot-breathing   erect, at ease, catastrophic
               harsh waves of stink, the
        dense air clogged with its roaring and
           ripples of power fork through us:
     hair gone electric   quick
             pricklish glissando, the
    skin   mind skidding, balking is
                HAIL
and it rears foursquare and we are jerked and owned and
               forgive us   and
        brought to a welter, old
    force & destroyer and
            do not destroy us!
      or if it seems good,
         destroy us.

     Thus, the god against us in clear air.
             And there are gentle gods –
           as plain as
       light that
             rises from lake-face,
     melding with light
that steps like a skipping-stone spatter
           down to
       evoke it,
     till blue embraces blue, and lake and sky
             are miles of indigenous climax –
   such grace in the shining air.

    All gods, all gods and none of them
            domesticated angels, chic of spat & wing,
     on ten-day tours of earth. And if
   to speak of "gods" recalls those antique
        wind-up toys, forget the gods as well:

tremendum rather,
dimension of otherness, come clear
in each familiar thing – in
outcrop, harvest, hammer, beast and
caught in that web of otherness
we too endure & we
worship.
We lived among that force, a space ago.

Or,
whirling it reins into phase through us, good god it can
use us, power in palpable
dollops invading the roots of the
hair, the gap behind the neck,
power to snag, coax bully exalt into presence
clean gestures of meaning among the traffic of earth,
and until it lobs us aside, pale snot poor
rags we
also can channel the godforce.
Yet still not
abject: not
heaven & wistful hankering – I mean
the living power, inside
and, that sudden that
plumb!
We lived in such a space.

III

I do say gods.
But that was time ago, technology
happened and what has been withdrawn
I do not understand, the absent ones,
though many then too were bright & malevolent and

crushed things that mattered,
and where they have since been loitering I scarcely comprehend,
and least of all can I fathom, you powers I
seek and no doubt cheaply arouse and
who are you?
how I am to salute you, nor how contend with your being
for I do not aim to make prize-hungry words (and stay back!), I want
the world to be real and
it will not;
for to secular men there is not given the glory of tongues, yet it is
better to speak in silence than squeak in the gab of the age,
and if I cannot tell your terrifying
praise, now Hallmark gabble and chintz nor least of all
what time and dimensions your naked incursions
announced, you scurrilous powers yet
still I stand against this bitch of a shrunken time
in semi-faithfulness,
and whether you are godhead or zilch or daily ones like before
you strike our measure still and still you
endure as my murderous fate, though I
do not know you.

PART III

EAST OF THE MOMENT

Somewhere east of the moment, the
gist of a radiant here and now
awaits its advent.
It is not apocalypse.
But in that
ampler place, which is
never fully extant for always it flares in our lives and then
gone again –
in that saner place, and yet
the image of where we live: same
job, same folk, same gritty
streets and destinations – somehow in that place
the things of day to day
coincide with themselves, they
graze at the source, in their ordinary traffic they are permitted
to move to a resonant measure, and a life-size
radiance prevails.
And not to dwell in that itch and intermittent glory – what needless
diminution.

COMING BECOMES YOU

Coming be-
comes you,
little one:
rockabye world as you lie, and the great pang takes you in
waves.   Coming
becomes you.

With horses you come, with arabian
slather with jugular grunts and in
fretwork, in fistfuls, on Fridays we come in the
danger and midnight of horses.
Coming you come like a spill, like a
spell, like a spoonful of flesh in the
roaring, high on blood
ocean, come with your horses, you come to be played.

In after-
come, you nuzzle;
you nestle and noodle and nest.
And the ghosts in your eyes
do their long-legged, chaste parade.
Each time such sadness
hushes me: slow
ache in your gaze – nostalgia for
now, for now as it
goes away.   You're
beautiful, small
queen of the pillow drowse, and
rockabye world in my arms.
Coming becomes you.

Wide.   Wide.   And
wide as oblivion river –
anonymous in its billions, the
tide of the dispossessed
flows on through time and stays.
And how can we reckon such grief?
Some by famine.   Some by chill.
Some by tse-tse invasion.
Flows on and stays, for in the
economy of the planet a
docket of daily pain
is scrawled in the genes of most who are not stillborn.
Some by torture.   Some by
plague.   Whole populations
enslaved.   Or battlefield slabmeat, stacked in
giant steps to raise
great generals to glory,
and there is scarcely a pause to humans killing humans.
But facing that history tide of sorrow, blank and
wide as oblivion river, is it not
hardest that each anonymous fleck of demise
was one like us? Each sporting his
nickname; toting
her singular, wild desires; or
this child's eyes as it died, and the mother caving in.
And again.   Again.   And again, to the
billionth iota of pain ...
The imagination balks.
To glimpse the sheer scope of statistical
hell – and then, to distinguish
body on body on broken individual body – is to
enter a moral hush, wide and

wide as oblivion river,
till almost I could choose to not know what my lucky life is borne upon.
Except I must.

DOWNWARD OF ROSES

Downward of roses,
scumward of oceans of whales, darkward of stars:
deathward dimension of every substantial thing –

did you not have dominion enough? did men have to lend a hand?

AUTUMNAL

1 · This Highway

When the music gets it right,
when juice & groove align it's like a pauper born to plenty,
    born to plenty,
when it all locks in, the swoosh and underpang –
that's when the god begins to
    shamble out of rehab,
or dreams he might it's been so long so long so long so long so long so long so
    longing longs to long
for one last kick at karma on the road again,
    one more banged-up bitte at the brink of eden;
when the music says I do, that's when you scavenge thru your
    rolodex of awe –
tracking the god, the god, the god, stalking that hard-ass
blur on the lam on the highway.

2 · The Shift

The first time I heard r'n'b, it was on
Buffalo airwaves, beaming the Sound of the Hound through the dark.
I lay on the sheets in a sweat.
Was it Sam the Man Taylor?   Eddie Cleanhead Vinson?
I was fifteen, I got straight A's, I was set to become a minister.
But nasty, nasty, the slow hormonal strut came pumping
juice & bad intentions, doing the
all-night downtown prowl.
This was secret information.   Whiteboy meets the body.
And the news took hold of my life, as Radio Gonad
pulsed, and faded, and pulsed.
And I didn't stop loving Eckhart, or math, but goosed by the sax in the dark I
lay and I sweated.
I could feel the shape of the mystery shift for keeps.

3 · Winging It

When the god gets horny, he
really slings the blues.   *Woman, c'mere* on
     tenor   harpfuls of gimme   and that
slow electric strut –
one hand in a glop of nirvana, the
          other in D.
Whoo ... do you luuv ...?   The whole joint lifting:
twelve-bar beerhall mating-call reverb –
     winging it winging it.

But can this geriatric coot still
     seal the deal?

Dionysus with haemorrhoids?
Don Juan in Depends?   Fat

chance, my friend: fat freaking
        chance he'll ever hit that switch again.
Best he can do is
schlep back out to the boonies, cop a gig, and
        wing it one more time:
                still tracking the
earth-to-us vibrato, still sussing pure
        pussy, mayhem, flop re-
generations – still chasing that
    wild unplayable *good-*
            gawdamighty, tick-
ticking up ahead.

        4 · *They Recede*

My heart is old-school: it wants what it
wants when it
wants it – no matter how
gone the belovèd, how lost the
things it thought would last.

My far-off years & companions – how
fiercely I cradle them now.
But they recede.

5 · No Peggy Sue

When the god swung back to heaven, there
     was no Peggy Sue.
No ache of lake perfection north of Kahshe.
   No bop cadenzas, snagging ragged *oms*,
nor loons to stitch his heart to faraway.

        But what did he expect?
      Heaven was just like
   heaven: same old *blah*, but
         more so.   He pried his fingers open,
    steadied his walker, muffed a
           tricky Hendrix lick ...
    Working the tourist meccas, for
        peanuts in heaven.

And friends – friends, what friends? – it was all just
     faces,
just cookie-cutter angels with their lauds,
         their tra-la-lauds,
   as westward loomed the war-
lords, chopping hands to keep the beat,
   and stacks of skulls in pitted avalon.

6 · Different Now

This is the house where I began,
this is the yard I played in,
and this is the ditch where I broke my –
    But it's *different now*, it's

all so different now.
I used to live here,
but it's all so different now.

This is the house where my kids were born,
this is the park they played in,
and this is the bench where their mother and I –
    But it's different now, it's
    all so different now.
    I used to live here, but it's
    all so different now.

These are the alleys I roam at night,
these are my oaks and icons,
and this is the city I dreamed could –
    But it's different now, it's
    all so different now.
    I used to live here,
    but it's all so different now.

7 · The God in Autumn

One year, the god awoke
        in a place beyond
acclaim, beyond fast fame, beyond fond
            honorific irrelevance.
Nobody's shaman now, he was blessedly
        ex-,
a blip in transit, a
        spook in embryo sneakers,

and the sum of all he'd played or sung or made
was chickenfeed.
Only ahead, ahead, ahead – the
gig was onward.

But woe to the man who
touches the hem of *tremendum*.
The undermusic
rules; wherever he turns, it
besets him.   And the decades go by, and
new biomorphic lingo
shivers his ganglia, and he hunkers to
honour the beat but now in clunky, rheumatoid synch.
Angina wiring.   Glaucoma fuzzerama.
But there is no geezer clause.
For truly, the tingle of radiant being is flint, and a
mortal who heeds it must splinter or else be honed,
and the same stark fate awaits the one who persists and the one who reneges.

The god in autumn
sat, in-
visible at last.
The wind had blown, the
leaves had flown, his
cells were human;
that show was over.
But through the hush of dusk, the dusk
still buzzed with unforgiving wave-lengths;
and when they wouldn't stop, the man
picked up his crip guitar, and semi-
tuned the one string left, and –

Tell the ones you love, you
love them;
tell them now.
For the day is coming, and also the night will come,
when you will neither say it, nor hear it, nor care.
Tell the ones you love.
I have lost many who mattered, and I will say it again:
tell the ones you love, you love them.
Tell them today.

Nightwatch

NIGHTWATCH (I)

Dark house. Dark night. Stac-
      cato skitter of cans –
raccoons in the lane.
And a flutterkick gust in the curtains:
nudge of the warm spring air,
blat of a ghetto blaster.
     And I could be out loving it, I could be
king of the night with a sexy Mensa consort,
gunning my id around town.
Not chewing bile again, not stuck here
wired on whiskey vibrato
in the wreck of my fortieth year,
who never thought my life could come to this:
alone, in a grotty house, with a shitload of empties.

And yes, yes, yes, tell me anything.
Tell me they love me still – not loud but
so I believe it.
And again! There was a time
to plod and plod as though sheer 9 to 5 was all that mattered,
and those endless jobs were dues I had to pay.
     But also a time for my plans to come partway true.
Eight books; great kids; recognition –
                     and with that, poor jerk, I
choked, I flailed, I spun out into wildness.
As when one night a year ago I woke in sweat,
and my wife lay locked and dreaming,
and in a pristine vertigo I knew my life had come apart.

          Which is the
              thing which I

thought I would think about.
                    (Clink!
                                    bright
                    cubes in the whiskey jostle.)
                                    Talk about (clink) the dream of a
brand new life in marriage. Brave beginnings, at 22 our bodies like
                    birthday gifts: the headlong
        yes, for keeps and how did the thing turn toxic? to nights of
                    cross-talk and loneliness in a subdivided bed?
        Though not just the tiffs about friends; her
snaky times; my overwork.
For there were lies in public places.
Across a whole bright-eyed and pampered generation
somebody changed the rules – ancestral certainties
of faith, and work, and marriage,
mutating to life-style options. Values à la carte.
Full frontal freedom, with nothing intrinsic to be.
        And we did, we actually swallowed that guff – we thought
new paradigms came easy, we never guessed
there'd be a price to pay,
nor that we'd end up tearing strips off lovers and comrades.

So our long declension began, the years of
        trying to invent a he, and a she, and a marriage.
                    The way that,
                                    (clink) that
                    hating the lot of women, and fearing the roles of men,
                            she put her life on hold, and engineered
        small failures from great gifts.   Or how I
                    spun my wheels non-stop to keep from writing – finding new
                            hopeless causes, fresh make-work assignments,
for I could not let my calling happen simply.

        Yet in my driven sleep I harboured

hunger pangs, subversive dreams
that drove me out to snag a volt of
jubilee –
I have been half unhinged with floating lust and intuitions, and for
what I don't know.
So I am one who keeps the nightly rendezvous,
same chair, same glass, same tapes and
why was the woman so hard? Lemme
tell you why – I
goddam made her hard,
through years of sticking together to shield the kids.
(... Oh man! it could break your heart,
how they itch to leave you behind and still be your child forever.
Me too. I want that too.)
But that was a piece of cake, compared to the breakup.
What shitheads we became, until
in a venomous trance and, OK a twinge of relief we
set the date;
the pack;
the move to this stately abode,
and now sloping through months of survival,
stepping lightly, *cha cha cha*,
like a zombie on uppers.
Plus: the terrible pain of children.
And this I learned by living, and it has taught me
nothing I want to know,
except I will never inflict such pain on a child again.

Hoo, boy!
It does not make for a sculpted
dignity, squelching thru
catatonic days & nights, disguised as a
large damp bundle of needs.
Dignity?! Tonight I could take a

half a million heartaches – all those
                    cornball teenage anthems, every
            twangy hurtin blues –
                        shove 'em up my ear and call it home.
Shee-it: I'll give them dignity!
                                Goddam-the-
            biiitch heartache!   Kiiids
                            heartache!   Pickled-&-pissed-in-
        scawwtch heartache!   Twitch-of-an-itchy-
            crawwtch heartache!
                            Couth as a camel's armpit: the
                maestro of maudlin …

            The dark is like a drum,
        where fitful inklings coalesce and come.
                And up it starts again –
Kee-ristawfuckenmighty! let me
spew it out of my mouth: the wilful
amnesias of a criminal civilization, expunging
lakes and skies and species, retooling
genes and pesky folkways – unbraiding the
harsh and seemly dance of necessity
till high on our freedom we soar above creaturely protocols
for we are the ones who can fashion new laws of existing, hot hot
hot in the mind of America,
and in a glitzy thuggish time how does anyone stay in a marriage
when the one good left is the will of omnipotent ego,
and castoff partners litter the landscape like roadkill?

            Ten blocks away,
        the midnight freight slides by. My god, that
            perfect bruise of sound – and my
                gut elides with the summons:

Come soon, pore boy, come

sooon; come

change your life.

High lonesome

long-gone trainwheel blues, and a brand new self tomorrow.

But who am I trying to kid?
"Modernity Wrecked My Marriage" –
   that'll wow them in Reno.
"Divorce Case Shock: Sartre Named as Third Party" –
    there's a bleat with legs!
But what right did I have to be married?
It comes to that.
  For I, who am not a vicious man, was barely here
    for the ones I love.
   I lived in another country: my mind, or
      where my mind kept going –
   where something thrummed and
     myself was almost the music,
and the truer that place, the worse my dereliction.
  But the children paid the price.
Their cause-besotted father gave them
nothing to live by, and I see my darlings reaching out for sustenance
in the city of kicks and neon, who can neither respect me nor
suffer me to hold them, for they know
the botch I have made of my time.

And truly, I do not know how to move forward in my life.
What make-believe I clung to! That each new
task, new rush, new busywork obsession
could somehow fill the vacuum at the core.
But when did I ever
hunch down? stay close to the bone? obey the promptings?

Room fades. Night
fades. And *thwock* in the plexus it gathers:
got place to go, know
where. Pour me some real –
me, me, sheer me of the universe!
And here, in the hush and slow dissolve, walls
buckle and hang and collapse. Dust tangles with gyproc detritus
till ribs of the building stand tall, they turn to
dance me, dance me off my entropy leash.
Blowtorch pariah!
Am lonely volt in the stone-cold mind of jesus.
And will not stop till find a point to stand on, for
I would rake out my eyes to get clean, get clear to
Danger: no return.

And the high goes higher, in an
exultation of undoing I abjure
all shelter, not one messiah shall shelter me. Let there be onslaught and
demolition of selves, pure
yaw of foundations, overhead cave-in to blackout and ambush of stars,
till space expands in my veins, goodnight, good-
night old life and I shall be large, be
large in the dark over Asia – spiralling out
with a hue, with a man, with a
cry with a human
cry, exist me to welkin, to firmament haemorrhage come,
wide in the slippage of time and
earth on your errands, far darling go
greenly, little planet survive for there are goths among the millennia.

SOMETHING ABOUT A TRAIN

Bright sunshine I must've, I
slept in my
lordy the clothes.
                    This room looks
totalled in daylight: who would have thought
the nesting instinct could suffer such epic defeat?
Something about a train, I remember a freight train.

And hello, little naked brain-box,
shivering on the rug,
wagging your plucked and pimply wing-
things;
            hullo, you pink
replica;
            hallooo! little
soft, moronic, too-too-frisky omelet – no
fling-&-fetch today; just c'mere, just
act like a goddam mind ...

Gifted with legs. With lungs. With a
luminous plash of sun on the
grain of a doorframe. Gifted with
time, which ticks. With a job I loathe. Gifted with
no more place to hide.

(And about my life: there was something about
making a change, and a leash and an
impasse,
            holy holy thud ...

BLUE PSALM (I)

                    Keep low, my
                              life.   Be still in the
          cardiac sessions, small when the
                              cornerstone gives.
                    I am not my self, I'm
          foreign goods – things own me,
                                        I know that now.
                    Keep low, little life.

                    Nicotine owns me.
                              Cholesterol too, and the sweet deadly
          booze owns my body.   And in my mind:
                    money, security, fame – how many non-stop
          compulsions repeat their
                                        imperious tics in my ego?
                    Even the dream of no-ego, of
                              goodbye desire: it binds me and owns me.

                              And,
                    beings: teach me to be.
                                        Not crouch like this, in
          cobbled time, in stigma.   Not
                                        freak on a leash. Nor
                    listless in slavery trudge,
          captive, abroad, and mouthing the alien tongue ...
                                                  Yes, and the
          unstrung harp hangs high, still dreaming what
                              dirge? what rage? what wind-borne snatch of home?

BLUE PSALM (II)

Hush hush, little
wanderer. Hush your
weary load.   Who touched down
once, once, once in America –
and over you flashed the net!
And they said, You will forget your name and
your home and
it was so: already I had forgotten.

But how did I come to be here?
This place is not my place,
these ways are not my ways.   I
do not understand their
consumer index; their life-style options; their bottom line –
weird abstract superstitions, and
when I settled in to stay,
it felt unclean.

But that was a life ago.
For I flourished, I
paddled in silks; I
wagged my tail for pay.
I poured sweet liqueurs on my tongue, and cried,
Here's to the old ways,
here's to our roots.
What have I sunk to?

Though they hem me with filigree,
this is not my country.
Though I bask on a diamond leash, it is not my home.
But what am I doing here still, how long will I

desecrate the name?
who was born to
another estate, in a
place I have nearly forgotten.

NIGHTWATCH (II)

Back with the scotch in the dark – how many
nights this way, old pal?
Lost in a judgement sweat, the rocky
tapes & jeremiads and around it goes again: Y' *gonna hafta*
serrve some-body, thankin
yew Mister Dylan.
    But it's out past words, to the thrash of calamity midnight,
where the bass line skids like a whip, like
acetylene balm, like a liquid wisp of forever and
what am I being?
Lost in the dark, with a slam-bang case of extremis.
Lost in my molten body, a Molotov handful and from this moment I swear
I can change! I can change! tip it
                over and momma keep smokin that bitch guitar.
       Got a cache of christened bullets, one for each
            pygmy self that lessens me, *crack!* – and
     tonight, tonight I'm contagious, tonight I could
           peel the lies out loud.

So. The smirk of possessions expires, in a flatulent cackle –
and what did I think, that a man could be saved by commodities?
I swore it wasn't true but the gadgets and gizmos pour
through me, buy me off
easy, wave upon wave in the headlong race to thing heaven.
    And payoffs at work dissolve:

twenty years of editing and for
what? a few good books and comrades aside, to drudge in the sewers of ego,
of back-biting, back-scratching, spleen, and all to
speed the canonization of mediocrity as a national literature –
was that worth half my lifetime?
    And applause of my peers dissolves, glad
hand of the also-rans;
I hankered for kinship but the tribe was founded on lies, and
dissolves the fellowship of failed ambition, bonhomie of
bile and wised-up ideals and how often I too went
whoring after approval,
forsaking the bedrock claim of the real for a mess of recognition,
the trophies of sellout.
Old shop-worn camerados, who am I to judge you?

                So, year by year and
                        numbed by success I went
                    wired to sweet-tooth mirages, till finally
        shucked & plucked & dismantled I
                    hunker at last in my body,
            and if there is even the ghost of a resonant I in the
                        blah-blah ego brigade I
                cannot locate it, and lucid and pissed in a small room,
                    how have I come to this?

And the dream-on salvation sorties dissolve, flukes of
auto-hypnosis and causes I leeched on, dissolve my vocation of
nurture for often I used the quicksilver empathy leadings to
get myself liked, and
dissolve and dissolve this knee-jerk curse and litany of dissolution –
I have collaborated in the falsification of my life
till spinny in gone light often I howl in myself, call down a
lethal wrath in the veins, move on, move on,
oh mother mother was it for this you bore me?

and this I achieved in Canada, where I came by
generations of flesh and methodists to lucid dead-end,
though once I was whirled about and gorged on the
rumours of God I reached a voluptuous
make-believe, but better now to
drink the night to the dregs than drift in anaesthetic glory.

But I will say this.
It was
heart's largesse, to have lived a space on earth.
How precious the rain. And the pines. And the
night winds too, they were precious,
combing the houses' hair.
I have stood hushed to the quick, tethered by
rockface and outcrop – mute jut of
molecular non-intent.
Or slash of raw sumach, scarlet past
scarlet in mind. And the merest
cloud changes, ten trillion per hour.
Everywhere, everywhere the harsh stark exquisite
tug of creature adherence;
I am no wilderness scout but there is a bodily homing which
I too was permitted to know.

But it's back to the shame and the
scotch, for as a citizen I
reneged. While my city slid to manhattan,
I stood by and clucked. And when the country, my beautiful
gutless Canada, lay back
and spread for a star-spangled buck,
in the time of the great betrayal, Mulroney ascendant,
I signed a crummy petition.
And as we went

lurching towards apocalypse, old
mother adieu in the cradle and starfield of eons,
I wrote some cheques and hoped it would all go away ...
                    Tippytoe! tippytoe! I may not know what
        human is, but I can say No;
                I can say No to you, and you with your ostrich denials and
deeper, bury me deeper – I can say,
                    Creature world, extinct;
                            I can say, Planet go nuclear come. And
        deeper, wedge me down deeper, nobody has to see me;
pretty please, just a little bit deeper ...

But when did it all go by?
The scotch is gone. My body's shot. And the years come
faster now, year by year they come
                    faster and
            pass me with their cargo of phantom aches and coronary alerts.
                I have squandered whole decades, it's
late too late to start and yet too
soon to pack it in and one day, bearing down
as the pain or the drug allows, half-claimed already
by the long goodbye and leakage of the grave,
what will I have, that rings true?
"You're born; you jack off; you die – what
more, little window-shopper?"

                        Sweet jesus, it's
            hard.   Hard to
                sit and accept – There is nothing more to imagine,
                        right now is my life; and also, how
            empty the night gets.
                    Night after night it gets
empty, for I keep
                trying to heed the voice, and follow, and

yes –
but then there is nothing to hold,
and nobody holds me ...
How late I reached the place of no excuse.
How late I learned to ask, what does my
animal heart require?

But tonight,
in the lash and ebb and echo of the music,
the years and years a shambles, every
goal I chased a bad taste in my mouth – tonight
let it all go by, and carry me home.
Just let me
cease with honour once, where silver
birches tumble back to compost glory,
blood of the hunted recedes,
tall buildings tilt at last to their bed of
gravity, old men their deaths and benedictions – all my
failures corkscrewing gently to rest, absolved,
absolved in the entropy pull,
for each creature is allowed its
downward momentum, and it is
seemly to lie in the place of oblivion.
Let me go home at last, and
if I do not rise again to the daily grind and betrayals, still
all will be well, and the
night will be well, and every
journey into endings will be well.

ONE MORE MORNING

One more
morning, god can I
fake it? Out the window: yards of blue
sky in my eye, some kind of birds with their
yattatta birdcalls, dumploads of light on St. Clair and the traffic the
numbness the shakes.
And it's off to work we go, with a smile and a
nervous system.

But what a
scabrous passel of hash is a man
with a hangover. Host to
cacophony – as now, for while he ghosts through his body's doldrums
he also feels the reverb: last night still going off, the highs like
banshees in echo park; today's bad news to come
a backward-spreading bruise, the meetings and paperwork and
already it is too much, and day after day it goes on.

But last night I lay, oh man I lay last night
while the music spun out into healing,
and in that extra hush I saw – what
was it? – I saw that
we are the ones who need not be. And can only be once.
Born kicking. Raised in the little round
of sun-up and labour and sleep. And then phhht!,
and never to be again.
  And though there are different clocks for the things which are,
the poplars and Rockies superb in their separate durations,
yet we are all, all of us gifted with coming and ceasing to be
in the one-shot pride of our physical bodies, and
precious enough to die.

And as I lay intent the jangle of time went to
radiance, I felt the fizz of
my own life, my dear ones, the species and planets like motes –
quick indelible moments, of each thing being itself:
ping of our one-way glory, each quirky instant
alive in its intricate timbre, gusto or heartbreak or
rarer indigenous wave-length, each incontestable being
a whoop, a whoop! in the world –
and curled in myself like a foetus, I cried till I slept.

That was last night. And this morning
a vision and 50 cents will get me a *Star*.
And the light's too bright, and
my life's not right, and this should
not be the constant condition
in which a man goes about his daily ways in the world.

BLUE PSALM (III)

How late, my
life, will I
graze in the malls of America,
crippled by plenty?   How
long will I put off the time?

For years I thought I was
gold, gold in a
secret place – and
one day, incognito,
the prince my soul would come and steal me away.

Fairy tales! a blanket of

fairy tales!
But there are great uncaring
spaces, and the winds whip through from there and
pick us bare.

(Gingerly,
soberly,
home – in a
torrent of
riddance.)

And so I came to,
and I cried, It is time to get shy of America,
time to move out of here.
We do not need these burnt-out dreams infesting our lives.
I will quit them, before I die.

CADENCE

We know a place to be.
It is not the same
for all, yet for each there is
one subcutaneous claiming: the place we belong to,
where our humanness is home.   And it is more an
exquisite taunt than a dwelling, for mostly we scruff along
by scotching the hints and traces – and how should we
honour that place? It is hard enough to get by.
And there are places I love, but when I found the one that owned me
it was nothing I knew. For in my twenties, god help me I
blundered into a –
what? A luminous tumult. Where I went in my body's mind. Not knowing
what that place could be, yet sensing

swivel and carom and thud I called it
cadence, more flex than content and
us in it. Feeling its current
snake through my life like a leghold rumble of is.
Though all the words are wrong – the place was
not a "place"; and the going was not in my
"mind"; and I didn't "go" there – still,
tumble and source and
vocation, and in that hush and quake of almost-words,
cadence is iffy but utter, pre-emptive, you
come or you go but you
do not possess it. It is
given and gift, a daily grace of
what.   And
what I know of being claimed, and home, and thank you,
is drenched with that sojourn.

And it was there I spent myself, day after day, in my thirties, obscurely,
gone now, and it nearly took me apart
to weather the pang transitions,
for when I emerged half out of my gourd I was
nowhere, I could not find good
distance with others – craving too hothouse a
union or skunked from adrenalin crash and that
herky-jerky to-&-fro
abrades a marriage; I came unstuck; I got frantic I
went to live in career, for I could not honour the stillness
in worship or in words –
what claimed me, unfitted me. And then it deserted me.

Yet when I was present to presence
there was nowhere else to be, and when not
it felt like betrayal.
As tonight it does also.

BLUE PSALM (IV)

When first we came to this land
there was a promise   a beacon   a
city on a hill, white clapboard new
zion perpetual lookout;
and in the streets, a rhythm and deals.
Lashings of brave blue sky – of gunplay and God,
high on a noose of glory.
It took us in.
Cheap beer.   New paradigms.   And we came
pelting down the street
when we heard that dirty beat, crying,
America, land of pure real estate!
imperial vista!   republic of raw material!
America turn us to gold!

Now: grain rots in the inland harbours.
And far in the boondocks, the empire prescribes a regime
of famine & torture,
torture & famine,
while here in the heartland the immaterial senses
atrophy, grown over. Yet in the
generations of our captivity, we bragged of our miniscule perks;
in the years of our exile we
scoffed at the rumours of home,
crediting only, USA/America   USSR/America   Babylon planet.
Though in the end we stammer, Earth, green earth and
dying: in our
lifetime, maybe,
goodbye.

Mostly we have to keep low.
But also it's good to come to be hunger pangs,

taking the
shape sheer craving makes. And it will go
hard with those who have found their ease in America.
I will come out.
For there is a calling, nameable by silence, and a
track, a path of no-
going. There is an
exodus, though mainly
one by one by one.   *I will come out.*
Whose price is my life.
And though my tongue is blind, and I balk and have no maps I
will come out.

NIGHT SONGS

1

Over me, over
me, oak leaves.
Dusk thickens by degrees.
Be well, great headfuls of night,
above my commotion;
I will not settle now for less than everything.

2

The thing I was hot for,
I squandered.
And the thing I walked by, I
now crave.

Home again home
again – that's how
it goes, it goes
by and you long for the ones you could barely wait to tell goodbye.

3

"Yes" in a life,
like bounty in a rose,
occurs and goes –

season of
headlong grace, and
then goodbye –

and what remains is
afterwards, and
coping –

4

Electric DT's of late-night unfulfilment, riffs of
she by impossible she – why was it so urgent to stay
hobbled to eros highs and the exquisite, long-distance mope?

Oh man! It didn't have to be lived. It was
so much safer that way.

5

The day insists awhile. And then
lets go its fleabite promptings.
                    Small gnats unzip the dark.

And this is what it comes to.
Lone bone.   Mouthful of need.
        Hominid toddler.

But I will not scotch my wrecks and blunders past the season,
                    nor magnify my
        nought beyond its time.

6

A day and a
            day, and I will
keep silent; a
            day and I will praise.
                    Gonna knock these
blues around – you know the sun still
                    shines, the night wind
breathes my name.

7

Across the street, a clutch of kids
dissolves.   "G'NIGHT."   "G'NIGHT."
                    The scene could be unwinding
blindfold, in a memory overlay.

The trudge through brimful dusk; the yodelled injunctions;
             the cry and reply, *G'night*, becoming
    faint as pals recede, the way it did in June
                    a lifetime ago, on Dunedin Drive in Etobicoke,
    when I was a likely squirt with a headful of hunches,
              and that other dimension, the stillness, came sifting through.

8

Like an arm. Like a
              leg. Like a transplant.
    I thought it went on and on, until you
                   ran out of things to let go of.
          I never knew
                    the season of meltdown ends – and
        still, like a leftover leg you
                    slog on till you, inch-
                          wise you
             make it to *whew!*

9

Star in your eye, little inchling.
        Kickapoo nova:
    snuffed and begun.

10

The names, the names, the names
till the namesaying ends.

I could say tacit a firm:
light of a no-light.

But hunker the wordless, the nub.
Hunker and ear.

11

Waiters and bankrupts, cops and illuminati,
              Tories and Sikhs and depressives ...
      And I guess there's room
for a member-at-large on the sidewalk –
      a seeker without belief, who keeps
          turning around. Not knowing what
    fastens him this time, for the city comes teeming
      with scumbags and wonders, all cruising for
home in his heart and in the wide world also there are signs
        of glory extant, and signs of
      evil in control;
and he will never meet them unmixed, nor make them be one.

12

Full of aught, full of if, full of empty,
fraught with beginnings, and lucky to be alive –

nobody's child in the heart-held silt of the century:
ferry the greening and grief to bare-bones extempore home.

13

Words, words, words! How have I lived, if not by you?
Not by sense alone. Nor audible sounds, although I love them.
   It is the sub-linguistic
                    seethe – half veiled / half opening – you
dislocate me into. Which
           stakes me out, which lures me, I'm a
goner one more time. And you seize me and whirl me about, mute
        words I'm mortgaged to:
   my owners, my darlings, my own.
        To whom have I belonged, if not to you?

14

     Small breeze, high
         whispering oak leaves.   And I'm
here, a thankful live one.
        Tomorrow, new dues.
   But tonight there is
        nothing to prove; just wait, just
move in the night's warm body.
     Body of edges.   Body of
        stillness.   Body of breathing.

HUNGER

   Looking back – what made me run? What pushed me
        year by year by year
through all those loves and drafts and jobs and last-ditch causes?
   It was hunger. Hunger. And, deeper than every

nerve-end purr in the pleasure machines of the *polis*, it was
                    unfilled hunger. Though for what, I can't tell.
          Outside the museums, the names of the sacred no longer work.
              They say too much, they say nothing at all and
                          though it seems strange to me,
          I cannot find words to declare what my heart was hungering for.

                        For the old ones grew exotic.
                    Marduk, Loki, Vishnu –
                              amen of dispersal;
                  Manitou, Ishtar, Zeus –
                      rustle of here & goodbye.
              They have become a rare, achieved, and
          dangerous hole in the species, residual nothing,
                          the space a passing makes –
                  Yu Huang, Utnapishtim, Quetzalcoatl;
                  Persephone, Yahweh, God.

              For we rose. And thought. And trashed our sacramental
                              birthright.
                  But I have lived 42 years, and never once
                          have I inched beyond the safety of lament ...
          But that's not what I *feel*. It's a playful itch,
                  a volt of desire which
                          hankers towards what
                  God was a blasphemy of – never yet
              have I danced full-tilt with my secret appetite:
                          to live in awe.

                  To live, at last, in awe.
                          And I know, many reclaim that
              sanity at the margins, where our bodies still sense
                  the tang of indigenous meaning. Returning to

granite, to cedar and loon – old
amniotic siblings.
Or, catgut hosannas; held in that burnished ache of sound, how the
soulmeat champs and respires!
Even torture and graft provoke it, the outraged
sense of a justice we half belong to, half can't find.

But now we live
closer to zero noon, and what I know best
is the naked need.
To flare in the wordless dimension. To hunch in my
other name, that doesn't have
I smeared all over it.   Almost it hurts to let go.
But in that arterial stammer, my back to words,
the yen just breathes.
No storms of presence. My mind still yacks and fidgets.
But hunger hungers, and sometimes I am permitted to mooch in the nearness.

HEART RESIDENCE

That creatures are not enough.
Hawkmoth and tanager snag me; muskies re-
call me, though alien in weedkill; raccoons
with their savvy instinctual poise haul me back to earth and,
wired in their unwitting circuits, bobtail and carapace all
species invade me,
tangling my reified soul once more in the bone fraternity
of things that are born and die –
yet though I crave it,
kinship and diastole the
creatures are not enough.

And roots are not enough.   Such
bounty I came to! heart residence on earth, and I have loved
a patch of ground too well: confess, confess at
                    dusk each summer long how a boy stood
            claimed by the hush of the Shield – the slow dark
        blotting the pines, and across the fretted
lake the loons re-echoed, and the excellent chill of infinity
entered my blood to stay as I went on listening, went on
                listening.   I was practising my life among
    rocky companions, but the
                        place is gone.

People, I hear we are catastrophe.
I hear we are strangers here.   For though we
                    re-fashion earth in our image,
    though in our hunger to nest we disnify the real,
        I hear we have no home. No
            home but hunger.

And precious, precious the dear ones – but also, that
dear ones are not enough. What man has been
        lucky in love like me? raised in a warm, in a
                principled sprawl of a family; gifted with luminous
        friends, who make low-rent jokes and live their lives nobly;
and quickened by eros – hard in its seasons, but holy and
                gracias, rare woman; and children who fasten my heart.
    Yet what will endure in time? and whom do I own?
            Was I not given such
peerless companions that I might learn to say, in love, Not
        you, dear heart; nor you; nor you –
                go by?

Testament

UN

A little planet blues, for the   blues
deathwatch.
A season of rictus riffs.
(When schist prevails, and squamous
pinpricks of appetite
vamp to a second future — who'll chant the
mutant genesis? who celebrate
an aevum cleansed of us?)

I

In wreck, in dearth, in necksong,   inwreck
godnexus gone to fat of the land,
into the wordy desyllabification of evil – small
crawlspace for plegics, 4, 3, 2, 1, un.

≈

Mind, and a home, and a rupture: rupture
old mother mutanda.
Surd journeys to scrambled states of once.
Lymphflange and cowsprocket; neurotectonics; organs.com.
Contusions of slippage & sloppage & inconsolable
us, re-
formatted to the new.

≈

I want verbs of a slagscape thrombosis.   slub
Syntax of chromosome pileups.
Make me
slubtalk; gerundibles; gummy embouchure.

brainrays   Icecaps shrink in the brainrays.
Leaf protocols gone skewy, mind-to-
green ratios a
barbous disproportion.
Synapse events on the pampas, while
consciousness voids all over the bowl of sky.

≈

hydro   New signatures of loss.
Fresh spoor of extinctions.
Late atmo of
warmfront & hazmat hup-hupping.
Coastal was comfort but soon a new swaddle of no-go.
Oceans placental, but soon a new hydro of gone.

≈

shotgut   Shotgut and
starways. Liturgy
offal. Residue eyes. Down
down down in the
belly of, dank in the relict, un-
winkled & dree.
Taxiderm inklings of mineral mind in extremis.
Clubfoot hosannas. Exfoliate consonant prod.

Of the metrophysics of ice: slipaway
slip away, seaboard.
In Greenland, a glacial divide – and
last call for littoral cities,
slipaway Sydney.
London.   Manhattan.   Mumbai:
nostril meniscus, then ciao.
Or dykage, and stiltage, and humanoid critters
vying with dogfish for allsorts.   Slip-
slipaway Athens, Rangoon, sub-
aqueous fables of *was*.
Rio.   Vancouver.   Shanghai –
slipslipaway Buenos Aires.

Cumuloss rising.   History slop in the wash.

≈

Scribblescript portents unfurl, world-   pidgin
to, worldfro.
And to comb the signs, to
stammer the uterine painscape
in pidgin apocalypse – how now not
gag on the unward, the once-upon, us-
proud planet?

tap   Tap-tap the embryo spooks at the portals of *ego*.
      Gone-boy the party-hard hoots from the house of condamned.
      Too-tardy heroes, marching to/marching to drumbelow.
      Misters of techabyte fixit, where did the world go?

                              ≈

mayday   Snoozing to mayday – the
         eyes in the headlights are us.
         How long till
         brakeback skid? till
         autowhammy meltdown? How soon till nocan-
         wannavamoose?

II

Under the cloak of day, heroic
mutations.
Out of the is-
scape, the iffy human smear.
Anthropox rising. Eschatosclerotic rose.

genesis

≈

In gabbro, in arcady vitro,
hellbright ego.
In Olduvai, fester and eros.
And the teleo-
skookum surge to hominid dominion: what geocidal
grandeur? what germinal terminus schuss?

olduvai

≈

Toxibelle, mon
fleur de ciao:
rose of dis-
owning, you open in
ozone in shoah in nofold embryonics.
Lady of nichtlichkeit, you flower somatic, en-
tropic, dyschthonic, till
no thing is proof.

toxibelle

names   That the names will end, that the
naming will end, that
the undis-
claimable forceducts of *is* will
resume their
eddies of post and pre.

Disarticulations of the stilled will,
I hear you inching.
Syllabic unhitchings among the galactic nevermind.
Expats of the pax humana; susurration of
fingerless glyphs in the limbo.

≈

unsaying   And speak athwart the scrutable.
Grain of un-
saying, and how.
Past lingolock pitons, reopening
forte and stillshine: that
hail of, that howl of unmuzzled desire.

Scarlight, scar-
blight in the chronifrag of no-man's:
sublingual agon.
Rolled scarlight up the hill, got
crushed, rolled
scarlight up the hill.

Of palaeopresence. The extra
space around what is.

≈

Is – now
there was a word. Was
funnelforce eddy of
strut & incumbence; pelt
yenful; carnivorous *abc*-meat.   Walls
juiced with kinetic copula – now
shrunk to a nominal gloss.
(Who combed the wind with horses,
who grazed with aurochs;
who champed in co-domain.)

admire

Totting this
boulder, that cedar, this
street that square, tick by
tock by admire: to
be is a bare-assed wonder, and in the
lethal occasions of earth it hunkers blessed.

≈

tagalong

Tagalong
snatches, algorithmic
hums. You even wear gene
disguises. Little anti-
threnodic peeps, tell nix in the slurry:
some-
thing matters, no
matter how nano the known.

Earth in the end days: grief
I *gave good*
grief. How-
ever you knew me, a bible, a babel, a-
merican bauble,
thru plague & renewals by
cullkill & mitzvah and
on-again/green-again/gone-again always I
gave good grief.

Carbon to kittiwake, lava to gita
I gave good grief.

tame

How cleave to the skank of extincting? How
signify unday?
We named it, we tamed it, we
gutted & framed it – and
thar she be: clean-clean, with a soupçon of tsk-tsk.

Me dork among parsewords.   Me diss in the lexic.
My beat, subsyl-
labic inferno.

≈

bears

The one about the bears.
What oncely
meant, corona:
starlight star-
bright star
kucked & cacked, riddled & wracked it is the
used-uppedness at lost, at
last, heart-
lubber.

In scraggy lingo lost,   inlingo
high mean-
times petering, thickets of
glitch & scrawn:
split for abysmal, hopalong
underword, head for no exit,
grapshrapnel yore spelunking.
Fractal untongue.

≈

Hang-   hang-
heavy heart, how
crippled you venture. How
hobbled you roam. Into the wake-up and
die of it – hang-
heavy dawdler, dis-
consolate clinger: burrow & sing.

≈

Innerly, underly: empty.   innerly
Outerly, party on.
Godloss once was a time, but now the
times devolve in the timeless mind of Mickey.
This too was human.
Noman's diaspora. Epiphanic o.

ologies   Ologies foundle. Oxies disselve.
                 Wordscapes and what they abstem,
                 neo & geo & ortho,
                 relics and runes:
                 oncelings, trekking to gack in gobi pastures,
                 erstlings on baffin floes.

≈

beloved   In silicon gridlock, in
                 quagmeat extremis – *basta*, on wings of success,
                 still we snog through
                 sputum waste to
                 caramelize the Beloved,
                 riffle thru alley slop for a gob of awe.

≈

yip   Ex-
                 tinction warmup dues: feel the
                 mindmeat resist.
                 Pre-necro hush, bombbalm to the planet but
                 yip yap yip go the ostrich curs of the brain.

                 Bite down on un-
                 tology.
                 Nuzzle the brink of extremis.

Not tell goodbye.   goodbye
Not strum farewell to sweetgrass/tundra/icecap,
nor plink so-
langsyne wackadieu to ozone eden.

No whalesong kumbaya.
Nor lynx nocturne, nor
papagayo kissoffs.
Not toll goodbye.

So much is gone, so much is
set to go.
Not peal goodbye.
No geopalinode, no solo mio.

Just,
hush for the snuffed; for
us, anathema.

                        ≈

Flin-   excalibur
tinlyexcaliburlockjut.

Tectonic aubade.

exodus

Under the
thes, under the as, under the
unders –
old folds of *other*, ob-
structing our schlep to the warm & fuzzy:

slag in the heartcraw,
paradise named away.

≈

history

In cess, in dis-
ownmost, in ripture,
in slow-mo history cease,
in bio in haemo in necro – yet how
dumbfound how
dazzled, how
mortally lucky to be.

And the unredeemable names
devolve in their
liminal slouch to abyss.
I gather the crumbs of hiatus.

The blank where *evil* held.
The hole called *beholden*.

That phantom glyphs resound, that
lacunae be burnished.
That it not be leached from memory: once,
earth meant otherly.

≈

Deathbreath of the unbeholden.
Mouth of the lorn.
Mining for syllable
rectitude, you struck clean seams of
lesser, of lesion, of
pitted implacable least.
Homefree at last in a whiteout of shock & Seine.

trump   Because the pangs are poised to swarm the city gates.
         Because it was flesh-eating crime.
         Last throe of the dice, that echolalic dinger.
         The earth is in shock. You must bear it.

≈

familia   Dieseldown momma yr mutants.
             Pater in litho yr cum.
             Bittybear boomp you go
             woebegone/wordbegone/worldbegone
             allaway home.

≈

lungfast   Lungfast in
             ernity. Talisman flybys
             abounding, a-
             borting. And
             hitherly, thitherly, *nyet*: the
             nightly clips of specimen grit & torture.

Through
glittery templates of e-
merce, say cheese.
Peekaboo in the
global lobophony.
Locked pocks in the heyday of value-free, I
shush to their witness:
that evil is real.
Unassimilable. Inexpungeable. Undisownable.

desaparecidos

≈

In naughtsong apprentice. In no-
zone neophyte.
And the coldsweat futures collide, they
jockey for
pathophanic edge. No fore-
lore, only the
underthrum.
Only the fat-chance shitpant survival inhale.

nozone

home   Last call for a trashable planet,
bring it on home.
Bring it on *sotto*, bring it on
shockabye. Bring it on oil-
wise, soilwise, waterwise, methuselah –
memory holes in the phyla, and
bring it on home.

(If home still
has a home. If roots
still grope for rootedness. If
butcherama,
botcherama, wide-screen
world has not yet
metamulched what is.)

And farfew the habitat heroes,
bring it on AWOL.
Bring it on oilwork, soilwork, patchwork, be-
gin again – through
plagues of our fathers, blue
culpa.   And
bring it on, bring it on home.

V

Lost word in the   word
green going down,
husk of a logos,
crybaby word, out
dragging your passel of absence –
little word lost, why in the
demeaninged world would I
cradle your lonely?
You, little murderer? You, little cannibal dreg?!

≈

And are creatures of   noth
nothing.
I noth you noth we
long have we nothed we
shall noth, staunch in true
nothing we
noth in extremis, noth until
habitat heartstead green galore & species
relinquish the terrene ghosthold;
crumble to alphadud; stutter to rumours of ing.

trolling   Trolling for gravitas.
Sussing the parsecs, dowsing for
day-one *tremendum* – sizzle of
is in the thoughtsong.
                              And you
too, if possessed: luck-
lock into pingdots anonymous. You too, my
farhither posse –
exceed me; excel me.
Through droughts & ghost savannas,
don't let me founder.
Through critterly whiteouts, compadres –
                              with your giddyup
inkles of tecto-extremis; your urches, your
fewfuls of penance & laud.

Plea pleading, pretty-
please pleadings.

befalse

By rupture to open: shock of
creature/no creature; first
barrow first gonesong first memory lingo freight.
Euphrates and Nile.
First harvest first parchment retention; first
pogrom obsolute.
First lost & last.

Plea pleading: that
all my truths be false.

≈

Wordward, on mission, remiss.
Dime-
store dexterity, jittery praise –
lipsynching awe all the way to the grave of the unknown onus:
memory stutter; one smidgen, one scantling of thank.

wordward

floruit   Was a one, was a
once, was a nothing:
mattered and gone. And how cleanly

our *floruit* will fade into
moteflicker, starcycle, eddies of
gloryfit ex. Where

nothing will
sing of us; build on us; blazon our
hubris & only

≈

youwho   You who.
You who never, who
neverest, who
ever unart.
You who summon the watch, who
hamstring the seeker, you who piss in the wine:
with this jawbone this raga this entrail,
with this pyrrhic skiptrace.
You who egg, who
slag, who un, who

Lullabye wept as asia
buckled,
rockabye einstein and all.

One for indigenous,
two for goodbye,
adam and eve and dodo.

Fly away mecca,
fly away rome,
lullabye wept in the lonely.

Once the iguanodon,
once the U.N.,
hush little orbiting gone.

≈

Blind
light, blind
night, blind blinkers.
Blind of the lakelorn / of
lumpen / the scree.
In terminal ought and deny, indelible isprints.
Palping the scandalscript. Sniffing the
petrified *fiat*.

stone

Stone uppance.
Starspunk shivaree.

Conjoin me.

YESNO

Song sinister. Song   *song*
ligature:
sing counter.
Are there honks, are there glyphs, are there
bare alingual grunts that
tonguefastly cleave to the iflift of
habitat mending? the judder of unsong un-
sung?

VI

If it walks like apocalypse. If it   apocalypse
squawks like armageddon.
If stalks the earth like anaphylactic parturition.
If halo jams like septicemic laurels, if
species recuse recuse if mutti clearcut, if
earth remembers how & then for good forgets.
If it glows like neural plague if it grins, if it
walks like apocalypse –

≈

Blah-blah was easy, we   blah-
diddled the scrutable chunks;
whole hog was beyond us.

Bugspace &
chugspace ahead,
welcome wormlandia.

The birds con-
trive a nest. The wolves a lair.
Sheer matricide is rare.

Undernot rising. Bad
OM, the
holes in the wholly.

awk

Bottleneck countdown; logomelt
cri du corps.
Stuck ruckus of geodilations.

What foetal botch impends? What
natal *awk*?
What gene-flubbed
cargo from postmark netherly?

Walk soft, conquistador. Among your   bwana
teeming climes and species,
bwana, beware. No
brook is what it seems, nor
veldt, nor pampas.

Sahib, go slow,
tread light in the food-chain.
The cattle tick, the trout betray; surveille
the very air,
it stinks of ambush.

Bwana get back, the
stats are leaking!
Inside the palisade, chop-
chop your ownmost D N A is
flaunting injun spin.

And kiss yourselves goodbye.
Is pasha crash, is
genghis melt is
its of you defecting.
No shelter.   ¡Pasarán!

hope

Hope, you illicit
imperative, throw me a bone.
What sump, what gunge, what
sputter of itsy renewal?
What short shot
skitter of green reprise?

≈

ganglia

Combing the geo-pre-
frontal, scritch-
scratching for relicts of *yes*.

Giddyup, ganglia.

Skulldug, with sonic contusions.
Hushhammer riffs.

Still singable   *still*
coleoptera. Still ozone
ave, still
redwoods memorious: earth

clamant, earth
keening earth
urnal, earth
gravid with loss.

Fluke
crusoe on boolean
sands, heart-
stopt with elderlore – still

spackled with
plosions of
let-there-be. *In-
cipit* afterplanet.

chumps   Here's to destiny chumps for a change.
Rogue arthurs; geek
parsifals; flammable joans of *salut*. To
stumblebum gandhis.

Who but a bupkus
quixote would tilt at the corporate mindmills?
Who but a blunderling
underling hoot at the emperor's shanks?

≈

holdon   Homeheart, great loanheart,
hang in;
blue planet, hold on.

Are scouts of the aquifer perilous –
ownheart, hang in.
Marsh templars. Heroes of tall grass resumption;
geodyssey samurai.

Not fold, great homeheart,
hang in.
Hold hard in the septiclot thromb of extremis.

And noful the species lacunae the alphazed shambles,   noful
but yesward the clearwater improv & biogrit slog,
and noful the corporate borgias the aquagoth vaders,
but yesward the stewards emergent in homewhether stab,
and noful chromutant the decibel swoosh of warmwarning,
but yesward the jiminy wakeup to planetude lost –
and noful-but-yesward the herenow & bountyzip nowhere.

tarbaby

Shucking our way to
us, in the crannies of impasse:
tarbaby toughlove.

Sloughing the fossilfix,
kicking the oink of the oil.

Nobody owns us. Nobody
owes us. Pork riddance.

Oofage & offage &
downboy.
Gravity prod.

≈

bambino

Dream on – of
bambino returning,
pox abated,
of scarified urchin-come-home.

Dream-on of bambino regained.
Wildward the
clearcut, oceans umbilical,
ozone declension on hold.

Bambino bambino, in
toxiholic recoil.
Escapist sanities.
Dreamfast, or nought.

As if a day more   asif
diurnal, a night more
maternal, a planet more
chockful of plenum & wonders still dawdled ex
mammary / machina / magica,
poised for a last-real comeback.

≈

And it falls like rain.   boom!
And it signifies like plague of indigenous nada.
And sluffs the everlocal yoke of is, while
gaga savants plot prosthetic fixes,
and noli tangos glide the lie fantastic, and
debit, debit, debit moans the moon –

telling how speakspace
puckers. How it
swivels and clots & ka-
boom! Percur-
vations in meanfield. Skewed
mentrics. Bunched losswaves. Impromptible knots of rebeing.
Rosetta palaver, unclued.

whistledown

Cold kaddish. In majuscule winter,
whistle down dixie to dusk;
coho with agave to dust.

Bison with orca commingled –
whistle down dixie. With
condor to audubon dust.

52 pickup, the species.
Beothuk, manatee, ash:
whistledown emu.

Vireo, mussel, verbena – cry
bygones, from heyday to dusk.
All whistling down dixie to dust.

≈

oompah

Pitch lumen. Crag
nadir. Sag tor.

Old icons go blank on the
dial, and the cumulo litter of *was*
exfoliates,
oliates,
oompahs the local to pulver.

How hew to the
pushpull? How
straddle the twain of what is?

How surd a blurward stut. How   *ave*
peewee thingsong,
surfing the plenary killcurve.

Barbary whoopup;
snatches of contact *ave*.

And borbo of cacahosanna: of smew of
beluga of animavegetal pibroch –
mixmuster of raggedy allsorts, syl-
labic in habitat soup.

Gumbo of
arkitude flotsam.
Flicker of
legacy toddlers, of
oldsoul avatar orphans.

oomph

Earth, you almost enough.
Hoof-high to excelsis, trilobite
sutra, cordillera jackpot:

into the new of attrition, the
birth of the lopped.
Into biosaudades.

Too fell a fate, greengone
inheritor;
iotacome donner & ooze – still singing,

Hail to the unextinct,
oomph to the lorn-being-born.

Mid-   twin
mortem the greenly; mid-
greening the renaissant thud –
mixmatrix our motherland.

Grammars of outcome,
twin-
twined in collision/collusion.

In plenody, threnody, whenody,
snatches of
gracemare.

Bipsychopathways.
Ontonot denizen splat.

≈

No DNA for the crunch – we got   DNA
neural nothing.
No yesno receptors; no template for cosmochaos.
No filter for earthly redamption.

Make me
cortical skootch in the trackless.
Amygdala vamp.

Sing me
synapse of hap and despire.

whatcan

What can, cog-
nostic with earthwrack, be
(who?ishly) known to co-
here, co-now with the
ratiosacral flex of
original yes?

≈

googoo

Whacked grammar of terra
cognita. Old lingo
aphasic, nuworldspeak mute
mutant mutandis –
                    fumbumbling what
aleph? whose googoo? which syllab? Test-living what
schizoparse of *am*?

High whys of   biscript
lossolalia,
one blurt at a time.

Wildword the bounty extant.

Is earthscan in biscript, is
doublespeak goners-&-hail. Still itching to

parse with a two-tongued heart, shambala
scrapings. To
praise with a broken art.

≈

There is a fuse. A fuss. A flex of intent: larrup
subsingular is on the hoof.
Radical larrup & given.

And it whiches, it
eachly enjoins.
Old dolittle spate.

To mark it, to
mark its incessance is
riteful as breathbone.

Halebent for
origin.
Creaturely mooch in the means.

avian

And avian farewells:
wordless in blinkerblank.
And nematode roads silting under:
hushmost palabras.
Cling to reverable, clang of no alibi, scrawk of un
uttered.
Of umbryo dicta, synching the lock-
jaw: [   ].

≈

amigos

Ace of my heart, a-
hoy!   Don't let me founder.
Glottis of varmints & *uh-oh*.
Sentry of parlous locales.

Blue who of bad corners,
wreckabye trekster – gone
geistmates. My
no-show amigos:

don't bail on me now.

Crashable brainscape: not   pinsteps
crash. Exo-
skeletal whir of controls. Of
controls! Of skidlock, of some-
body-stop-us.

By pinsteps to choreocrackup.
Vertigo yen.

Courting the
glitch in the hominid regnum; craving slop-
stoppage of clash & blurn.

≈

As stuttle inflex the genomes.   flux
As bounty floundles.
As coldcock amnesia snakes thru
shoreline/sporelane/syngone –
                              hi diddle
template, unning become us,
palimpsest gibber & newly.

I spin the yin stochastic, probble a
engram luff, & parse haw
bareback the whichwake, besoddle a thrashold flux.

tango   Calling all
lords of the rigamort tango,
maestros of entropy glide:
we're pushing it
to with an amazon shimmy, hoofing it
fro with a greenhouse fandango; little bit
closer with canopy kissoffs, little bit
farther with coral abrasions –

Stepping lightly, cortex courageous,
high-hats macabre: keep keep keep
pumping that critterly whiteout, goosing it
faster in biophobe boogie;
doing the
gainful extinctions con carny, towing them
bones in the geospazz conga –

Last call for the
champs of demise now:
one more
glug of that sweet intifada, one more
slug of the rictus merengue;
treading the
rockabye samba to notown, strutting the
kamikaze victory obit –

Bellyful:
burnout is
best.

[   ]

back

Baby come back. Come
easy come queasy come faraway-willaway,
bonehead electric like big boys but
baby come back, breathe
deep in the motherlode. Dumb
kopf in a sling & come broken,
baby come home.

≈

fold

You fold you are
folded, late-breaking primate, and
brought to who-knew.
Fold you are
null again, nil again, knell again – one-swat no-
see-um & whose.
Stud of no
throne no dominion, kingshit of doodly.
Frag in the mean of let-be.

Earth heres, earth   listen
nows, is there
nothing?

What whats?
Inlisten.
What quickens?

Inner than
polipulse, homer than breathbeat, listen to
isten. To

istence. Listen to inguish. Listen to
is.

diggity

Deep
is, and be
struck. Be stricken.
Be amnioflex of the daily, as
things wriggle free of their names,
subsist in
sheer diggity *fiat*.

Be wild & be-
wildered.
Undermilk arbour, arbourmilk under –
sesame endwise:
stillwill and re-boot.
Squiggles of *ing* on a
field of native null.

Herk lurch to
protobang –
quotidi-/
aeonic ah-
ha! What comes
to be is
beholden.

Was HIGGS; was BANG; was URBOP. Was
max in a smidgen. Was *is*.
Googols of firstforce. Itch rhythming –

still rampant in lichen & esker,
aphid & tanager. Still
startup in coral & smee.

Gimpalong beauties. Fucked
fractals of ogeny sprong.

≈

What we sniff/palp/schmeck/wrack/
ravish, but
can't commandeer. The
plosive being of beings.
Quickquark the ammonite, cognate the andes;
gratuitous stakeouts in time. Each a
fleck of first-day durance, a
fluxy reverb,
sheer chronojolt & onwards.

Thrum of material kickstart.
Jiggers of genesis.

bandwidth

Hope without
bandwidth.
Itch without mouth.
Deepsong gone long-gone, gone not-yet to ground in a
flurry of *shhh*.

Newful the needful – re-
boreal peeps in kaputski.
No north, no south, just yenway.
Just, hunkerdownduly & looselip a blurt of begin.

≈

stinct

Which thing is us.
We of the
waste-deep the
westering, we of the
cackabye outstinct on ice.

And are bodily implicates.
Are denizen-drenched, self-x'd,
are phyxiate foundlings,
woozy with birthright and
laced with caterwaul *rerum*.

Clamber down babel, climb down to the
nearaway country of homewhere. Of
bastard belong.

At the still open grave of the   *forgi-*
not-yet-write-
offable cashcorpse –
blindblabbing our
gobshut, our
gutted-by-greenslag, our undisad-
missible burden: *for-*
gi-   forgi-

In morituri funk.

                                    ≈

Body of primal, body of   survive
plumb: it is to
you we owe our being,
carne of undergone epochs.

Destructible mother, survive us,
widewinnow our folly.
Foregather, in interlore
rehab agon, our
little, our lustral, our late.

abc

Of more the less; of
least, prognostipangs.
Scrabbling for *abc*.

No heaven, no
beanstalk, bare earth.

Shedding what pyrotech-
tactics?
Threading what speakab/un-
speakable, ekable, seekable
gauntlet of need?

≈

tilth

Terragon tilth, or
heartwork in kinderpolis.
To couch in the knit of the sinew, to
ponder refoliant scrub.
To gawp at what thrives without us.
To jimmy the civil equations, resetting for
osteo clicks of alignment,
onus upon us;
salaam to what heals
in the real.

Extempore if-
space & greening,
plant heartflag here.

extemp

Thru witslog, thru willslog to
glimmers of thingdom come;
pitch soulhold here.

Labour & claimstead – of
inchables,
karma oscura.

Staking the bundle. Brought,
broke, to
indigenous *fiat*.

≈

Squeaks from the sisyphus chorus.
Hums from the crunch.
Dopey & grumpy & doc, just
truckin along –
here come chorale;
mind to the
grindstone, ear to the plough.

dopey

Hi-
hoein along with a song:
What home but here? Whose grubby paws but ours?

yesno

With a *yes*, with a *no*, with a
yesno;
sonics in simuljam.

To habitate crossbeing.
To ride both reals at once. To least-
wise stay
vif in detritus/un-
lulled by the blessingbait green.

≈

demesne

If inly, if only, if
unly: heart-
iculate improv,
sussing the emes of what is.

Nor hunker in losslore, nor
kneejerk abracadaver.

Cripcryptic rejuice! Ec-
statisyllabic largesse –
rekenning, rekeening, re-
meaning our wordly demesne.

Grunts from the trench, the killzone: mutt
peeps from the front.

Lithoslag / bioslag / noöslag –
hasta la omega.

Ciao to the caesarly, bye to the kaiserly, howdy
grim repo.

Hemis of brokensole. Demis. Mutt
angelus minims.

galore

If hope disorders words, let
here be where.
Lingotectonics. Gondwana nar-
ruption vocale.

How can the
tonguetide of object/sub-
jection not garble what pulses in
isbelly?

Nearflung & thingmost, re-
tuit sheer carnival logos. Where
nouns ignite
moves in the dance they denote:
moniker lifelines.
Cedarfast. Willowpang. Maplemind.
Oakable homing, notched in the bone.

Only co-
phonic. Co-
founded. Cofoundered.
Only galore.

Mercator cleanup or what?   orwhat
Toxijam loosened, slum-
praxis goosed;
techmate relievo or what.

Alphas of stricken, bare omega noodlers –
swot to revivify human,
vamping on taptoes of must.

By the law by the lab by the ballot:
sanity sweat.
Lost-ditch endorphins or what.
Hometruth cojones. Or what?

tale

Tell me, tall-
tell me a tale. The one about
starless & steerless & pinch-me, the
one about unnable now – which they did-did-
did in the plume of our pride, and
could not find the way home.
Little perps lost.

Yet a rescue appeared, in the
story a saviour arose. Called
limits. Called
duedate, called countdown ex-
tinction/collide. Called, eyeball to ego:
hubris agonistes.

Bad *abba* the endgame. In-
seminal doomdom alert:
pueblo naturans, or
else. But the breadcrumbs are gone, and the
story goes on, and how
haply an ending no
nextwise has shown us, nor known.

AUTHOR'S ACKNOWLEDGEMENTS

Many friends and editors have helped with these poems over the years, and I thank them warmly. With special thanks to Don McKay, *primus inter pares.*

I'm grateful to the publishers who brought out the work, and in particular to Anansi for proposing this *Collected.*

Linda McKnight and Hilary McMahon, agents *extraordinaires,* have been beacons of sanity for many years.

The patron spirit of this volume is Robert Bringhurst, who put his prodigal talents as poet, editor, and designer/typographer at its service.

The dedication expresses my beholdenness to Susan Perly – a fearless writer and reader, and the love of my life.

D.L.

EDITORIAL ACKNOWLEDGEMENTS

The text of *Riffs* is taken from the edition of *Riffs* published in 2015 as Brick Books Classics 2. It is reproduced here with the kind consent of Brick Books.

HarperCollins Canada has graciously permitted the use of poems from *Alligator Pie*, *Garbage Delight*, *Jelly Belly*, *The Ice Cream Store*, *Bubblegum Delicious*, *The Cat and the Wizard*, *Garbage Delight: Another Helping*, *SoCool*, and *Melvis and Elvis*.

Lizzy's Lion was first published by Stoddart in 1984 and is reprinted here with permission of Fitzhenry & Whiteside, Canada, 2016.

Three of the four photographs facing the title page – taken in 1987, 1993, and 2014 – are by Susan Perly. The remaining photo, taken circa 1957 by an unidentified photographer, is drawn from the Dennis Lee papers in the Thomas Fisher Rare Book Library, University of Toronto. It is reproduced here with the Library's kind permission.

I'm especially grateful to Jennifer Toews at the Fisher Library, Lorna Chisholm at the National Library of Canada, and Susan Perly for their expert help with photographic and background research.

R.B.

KINGDOM OF ABSENCE, Dennis Lee's first book, is a series of
43 poems, each roughly the dimensions of a sonnet. The poems are
grouped into seven sections of varying length but numbered con-
secutively throughout. The work was published by House of Anansi
in 1967 in an edition of 300 copies.

CIVIL ELEGIES: The *Elegies* were first published by Anansi in
1968 as a book-length sequence of seven poems. Substantially revised,
they appeared again in 1972 as a sequence of nine, accompanied by a
group of 16 other poems. The nine elegies are reprinted here in their
entirety, with the minor revisions introduced in 1996 in the volume
Nightwatch: New and Selected Poems (McClelland & Stewart). The other
poems which appeared in the 1972 edition have here become Part I
of the section called "Not Abstract Harmonies But."

ALLIGATOR PIE: Poems in this section come from the two edi-
tions of *Wiggle to the Laundromat* (Rochdale College, n.d., and New
Press, 1970), and from *Alligator Pie* (Macmillan, 1974), *Nicholas Knock
and Other People* (Macmillan, 1974), *Garbage Delight* (Macmillan, 1977),
Jelly Belly (Macmillan, 1983), *Lizzy's Lion* (Stoddart, 1984), *The Ice Cream
Store* (HarperCollins, 1991), *Bubblegum Delicious* (Key Porter, 2000),
Garbage Delight: Another Helping (Key Porter, 2002), and *Melvis and Elvis*
(HarperCollins, 2015). Incidentally, the two editions of *Wiggle to the
Laundromat* arc distinctly different books with the same title. The
Rochdale edition bears no date but was probably published in 1967.
It contains 40 poems. The more lavish New Press edition, published
three years later, contains only 17 poems, not all of them drawn from
the original 40.

THE DEATH OF HAROLD LADOO was originally published as a
chapbook by Kanchenjunga Press in 1976. A revised version appeared
in the collection *The Gods* (M&S, 1979). Minor revisions were made
when the poem was republished in *Nightwatch* (1996). The version
printed here incorporates further revisions.

THE CAT AND THE WIZARD: Poems in this section are chosen
from the two editions of *Wiggle to the Laundromat* (1967? and 1970),
Nicholas Knock and Other People (1974), *Miscellany* (privately published,

1977), *The Difficulty of Living on Other Planets* (Macmillan, 1987), and *The Bard of the Universe* (Gaspereau Press, 2007). The title poem, "The Cat and the Wizard," first appeared in *Nicholas Knock* in 1974. It was revised for publication in *Other Planets* (1987). With further minor revisions, it appeared on its own as *The Cat and the Wizard* (Key Porter, 2001). The 1987 text is printed here.

"I DIDN'T WRITE THIS POEM BY MYSELF": The Hungarian poet György Faludy (1910–2006) lived in Toronto from 1967 to 1989. During that period, Lee and others joined in a long-running project to produce English versions of a selection of Faludy's poems. Lee worked from English prose cribs prepared by Eric Johnson, George Jonas, and Andrew Faludy. His versions range from the close to the decidedly free and interpretive, but all were approved by Faludy. They were first published in George Faludy, *East and West: Selected Poems* (Hounslow, 1978) and *Learn this Poem of Mine by Heart* (Hounslow, 1983), both edited by John Robert Colombo, and in Faludy's *Selected Poems 1933–1980*, edited by Robin Skelton (M&S, 1985). The Hungarian originals can be found in Faludy's *Összegyűjtött versei* [Collected Poems] (New York: Püski, 1980).

SOCOOL: All poems in this section are drawn from *SoCool* (Key Porter, 2004).

RIFFS: An early version of this sequence, consisting of 67 sections, appeared in 1982 in the journal *Descant*, as part of a special issue devoted to the work of Dennis Lee. (The issue was also published in book form by Descant Press as *Tasks of Passion: Dennis Lee at Mid-Career*, edited by Karen Mulhallen, Donna Bennett, and Russell Brown.) A fuller version of the poem, with 88 sections, was published by Brick Books in 1993. Lee made a number of minor revisions when the sequence was republished in *Nightwatch* (1996). The *Nightwatch* version of the text was published separately by Brick Books in 2015. With a few minute adjustments, that version is printed here.

THE MOUSE AND THE MAID first appeared in *The Difficulty of Living on Other Planets* (1987). The version published here includes some new but minor revisions.

NOT ABSTRACT HARMONIES BUT: The poems in Part I first appeared in the "Coming Back" section of *Civil Elegies and Other Poems* (1972). Part II is drawn from the chapbooks *Not Abstract Harmonies But*

(1974) and *The Gods* (1978), both published by Kanchenjunga Press, and from the larger collection also entitled *The Gods* (M&S, 1979). In Part III, the "Autumnal" sequence is new; the other five poems come from *Nightwatch* (1996).

NIGHTWATCH: All the poems in this section originally appeared in *Nightwatch* (1996), but the two title poems have been substantially revised.

TESTAMENT: Sections I–V of *Testament* were published as *Un* (Anansi, 2003). Sections VI–X were published as *Yesno* (Anansi, 2007). The entire sequence was then substantially revised and issued as *Testament* (Anansi, 2012). The full sequence is reproduced here. The typographical arrangement is new, but the text is fundamentally unchanged from 2012.

R.B.

¶ In this index, the titles of poems and sections are in italic; first lines or opening phrases are in roman. When the title and first line are effectively identical, only the title is listed.

□

HEART RESIDENCE was edited for the press, designed, and set in type by Robert Bringhurst. The text face is QUADRAAT, designed in the Netherlands in the 1990s by Fred Smeijers. The titling face is COMENIUS, designed in Germany during the late 1970s by Hermann Zapf.

□

□

□

DENNIS LEE was born in Toronto in 1939 and has made his home there ever since. In more than half a century of active literary life, he has published close to forty volumes of poetry and prose. In 1967 he co-founded the House of Anansi, directing the press until 1972. From 1967 to 1969 he was also one of the leaders of the legendary Rochdale College, an experiment in self-directed higher education. He was consulting editor at Macmillan of Canada from 1974 to 1979 and poetry editor at McClelland & Stewart from 1981 to 1984. During that period, he wrote the song lyrics for Jim Henson's television series *Fraggle Rock* and contributed to the scripts of Henson's fantasy films *The Dark Crystal* and *Labyrinth*. His selected essays, *Body Music*, has become one of the cornerstones of Canadian literary criticism. His children's poetry, published in dozens of handsomely illustrated editions, has been adapted many times for stage and television and can be heard chanted by children around the world.

From 2001 to 2004, Lee was Toronto's first poet laureate. In that capacity, he initiated the Toronto Legacy Project, which marks sites throughout the city where notable figures lived or worked. From 2011 to 2015 he was a resident artist at Soulpepper Theatre Company, where he organized the "Lost Songs of Toronto" cabaret. He is married to the novelist Susan Perly and has three children and two grandchildren.